A GUIDE FOR
CREATIVES

FREELANCE, AND BUSINE$$, AND STUFF

Revised First Edition
By Amy Hood and Jennifer Hood of Hoodzpah
HoodzpahDesign.com

Quickened Publishing · Newport Beach, CA

Freelance, and Business, and Stuff:
A Guide for Creatives

Copyright © 2018, 2019, 2020 by Hoodzpah, Inc.

All rights reserved. This book or any portion thereof may not be reproduced or used in any manner whatsoever without the express written permission of the authors except for the use of brief quotations, which must be correctly attributed. If you find errors in this text or have any suggestions for additions, please contact info@hoodzpahdesign.com.

Printed in the United States of America
Revised First Edition, 2019

ISBN 978-0-9847363-1-7
Quickened Publishing

Disclaimer:

This book is made up of our personal research and experience, and it should in no way be a replacement for professional legal or financial advice as every person's individual circumstance is different. Discuss your personal needs with your own accountant or lawyer to ensure you're making the best decisions for your industry and location.

How to start your own business, grow your client base, and promote yourself without selling out or starving. This no faff, no fluff guide is peppered with applicable advice (things we learned from starting our own business), unasked-for humor, and worksheets (homework, gasp!) to help you just get started already. Because raw talent and good ideas aren't enough. And because you can do this. Really. »»

WRITTEN BY:

Amy Hood & Jennifer Hood
Co-founders/Principals of Hoodzpah, a brand identity and
type design studio based out of Orange County, CA

LAYOUT BY:

Amy Hood, Jennifer Hood,
and Arturo Jimenez

EDITED BY:

The Inimitable Lindsey Bro

ILLUSTRATIONS BY:

Amy Hood

BIGGEST THANKS TO:

The "Bear," our Business Mentor

Thank you also to: Jason Staggs, for giving us our first chance at working as real designers; Liz Logsdon for dreaming big dreams with us when we were twelve; Grandma, for starting her own businesses when she was young, normalizing entrepreneurship in our mind, and encouraging us to penny-pinch; Austin, our cuz, for holding down the fort in Kentucky like a true warrior in baby blue scrubs; Dad, for bringing us to his construction job and including us in his fix-it projects - they made us industrious; Troy Puckett for unknowingly inspiring our first ever logo in 5th grade; Paul Hutchison for being a mentor without perhaps knowing it; Nick Slater for referring us to speak at Creative South, and Mike Jones for making it happen - this book grew out of that first conference talk prompt; Josh Ariza, Joel Beukelman, Mitch Goldstein, and Ash Huang for their discerning eyes on various parts of this book; Catharin Eure for giving us our first teaching opportunity, which helped us fine tune this book; Bea Morgan for being the best Assistant to the Regional Manager; Tara Victoria, Danielle Evans, Meera Lee Patel, and Kate Gremillion for lending their ears and advice throughout the process of making the book; and Arturo Jimenez for all his help with this book layout and countless other design projects.

www.hoodzpahdesign.com
Instagram, Facebook & Twitter: @hoodzpahdesign

There's nothing worse than a wedding hashtag.
Except maybe a book hashtag?
Tag us! #FABAS #Hoodzpah

Hoodzpah
SHINE ON.

Table of Contents

*	Introduction	*7*
1.	Do You Have What It Takes	*11*
2.	Get by With a Little Help	*23*
3.	Making a Budget	*31*
4.	Pricing and Proposals	*45*
5.	How to Create a Business Plan	*65*
6.	Branding Your Business	*75*
7.	Making It Official	*95*
8.	Growing Audience, Promoting Yourself, and Getting Work	*105*
9.	Contracts	*121*
10.	Workflow Mojo	*129*
11.	Communication and Collaboration	*139*
12.	Taxes, Accounting, and Measuring Financial Health	*151*
13.	Staying Competitive and Adaptive	*161*

Introduction

On a scale of 1 to 10 (one being easiest and ten being hardest), starting your own business lands somewhere between setting up a printer and teaching a teenager how to parallel park. In other words: it's not easy, but it's definitely not impossible. It really comes down to patience and hard work.

You truly don't have to be a genius to start your own business, and you don't need thousands of dollars. Heck, you don't even need a college degree. Best of all, you definitely don't need permission. But you do need patience and diligence in spades. Add a little common sense for making clear decisions, enough skill to do good work, a healthy hunger for knowledge, and a shake of pliability (adapting is key) and you're good to go.

DIFFICULTY METER

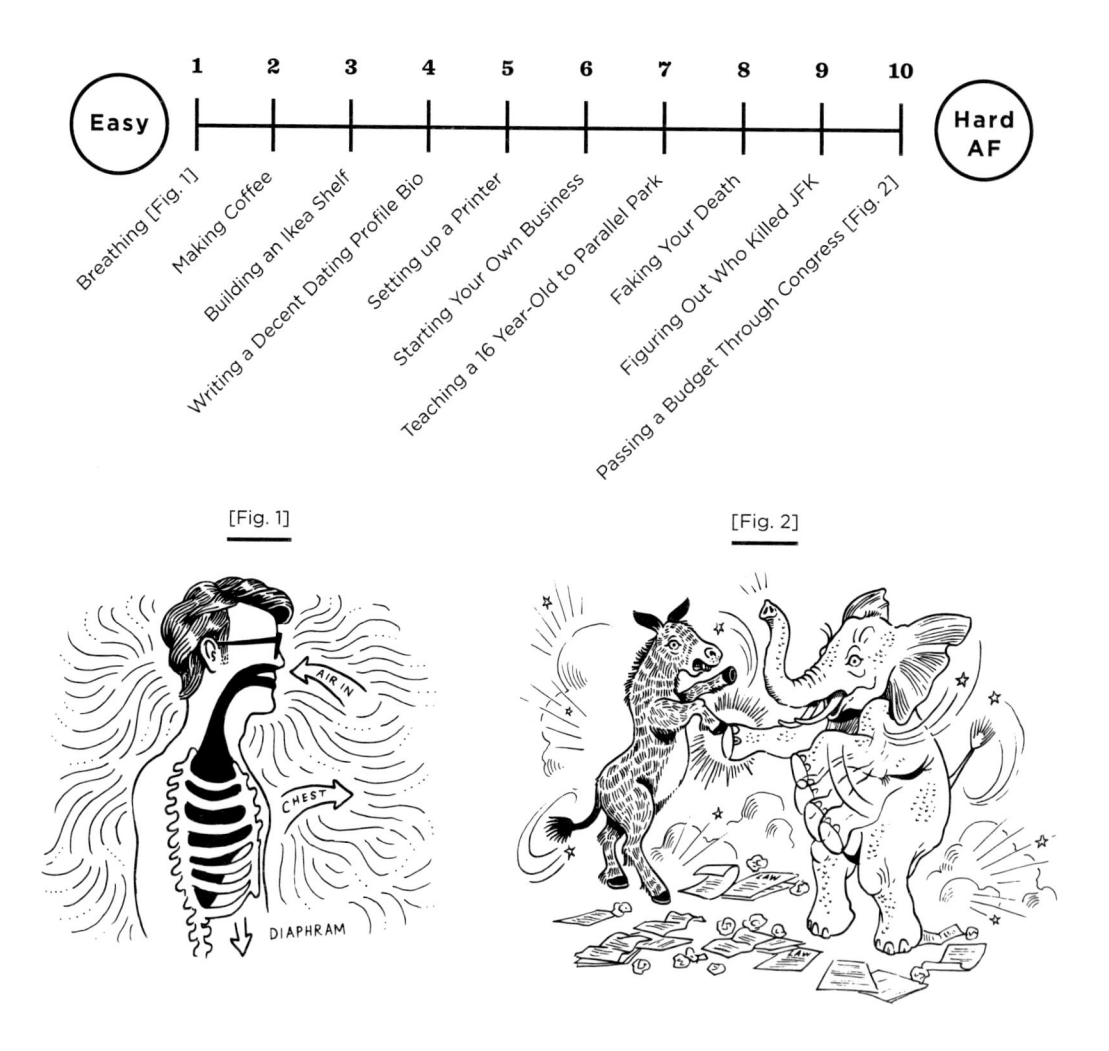

Easy — 1 Breathing [Fig. 1] — 2 Making Coffee — 3 Building an Ikea Shelf — 4 Writing a Decent Dating Profile Bio — 5 Setting up a Printer — 6 Starting Your Own Business — 7 Teaching a 16 Year-Old to Parallel Park — 8 Faking Your Death — 9 Figuring Out Who Killed JFK — 10 Passing a Budget Through Congress [Fig. 2] — Hard AF

[Fig. 1]

[Fig. 2]

#FABAS @HoodzpahDesign

According to the U.S. Bureau of Labor Statistics, about 10% of all U.S. workers were self-employed in 2015. Intuit predicts that by 2020, about 40% of American workers will be independent contractors. A lot of people came before you to pave the way. Remember this when fear starts to consume you. You aren't the first pioneer, and you're absolutely not alone in this. Our goal is to give you a simple roadmap with solid advice (both practical and personal) so you have a head start and can avoid making common mistakes.

Freelance can truly enrich your life. It can be a way to make side cash to supplement your income; to test a new profession or skill without ditching your steady day job; and to work on projects that fulfill you (if you're feeling stifled or stagnant in your work). When you run your own freelance or creative business, it gives you more power to choose how you work (when and where), what you work on, who you work with, and how much you make. The gain is more flexibility and control. The trade-off is more responsibility.

We hear so many people talk about how uncertain and inconsistent freelance feels compared to being employed by someone else. In some ways they're right. But here's how we see it: when you run your own company, you're much more involved in the decisions that impact its success. You have a hand in determining its future, rather than being at the mercy of your employer's decisions. We find more security in having this control and knowing the full picture of our business. Full-time freelance might not be for you. But we highly encourage everyone to try freelance at least on the side. It gives you know-how that makes you more hireable. You'll learn how much goes on behind the scenes of a creative company to keep it running. You'll gain a sense of your value and purpose beyond your day job, and it'll give you more confidence when it comes to negotiating salaries and landing better positions at work.

A Small Side Note: When we refer to "starting your own business," this means everything from being a freelancer to starting a company with employees and partners. Think of freelancing as a small business, party of one.

This book is a collection of things we've learned over the years from smart friends and mentors, to countless deep-dive Google searches, and good ol' trial and error. We've combined the legal rules of freelancing with our own best practices for doing business well. Our approach tends to be low-risk and low-cost, because we don't think you need tens of thousands of dollars to get things going. Best case scenario: you have a steady job while you try out freelance on the side. Wade in, take your time, and prove your concept. After all, why dive heart first into the world of freelance before you've had a chance to dip your toes? If things are working well, then go for it full time!

While we love our approach, we know it isn't the only way. There are a lot of ways to run a successful business and it comes down to your personal disposition, talents, experiences, finances, and needs. In our quest to find that magical spot between smart and sexy small business, we thought it'd be best to start with a checklist detailing everything you'll get done by the end.

Go on… turn the page.

Illustration by Amy Hood of Hoodzpah (Hoodzpahdesign.com)

1
Do You Have What It Takes?

A pep-talk plus the third degree.

———

We'd like to start by saying: dumber people have done this. Starting your own business will be clunky and unfamiliar at first, like a baby deer on a trampoline, but it's just new. You're building new skills in an unfamiliar environment. Fearing what you don't know or don't understand can only last as long as you let it. Don't let the inevitable missteps and mistakes shock or dishearten you. Expect them (As sure as the airport chase scene at the end of every romantic comedy movie, and as guaranteed as the tears of Adele). Don't beat yourself up when things don't go as planned or when a decision you've made backfires. Adapt and be patient with yourself as you find your groove. There's enough haters out there. Don't be your biggest one.

It's important to not classify every hiccup as a bad omen for your new endeavor. You have to put in the time to figure things out. Even after you've created a well-oiled machine, there are countless unforeseen wrenches on their way. Get over the fear of failure or the idea of perfection. The sooner you're ready to do that, the sooner you'll be able to focus on big picture problem solving. Plus, all those bumps in the road are exactly the kind of anecdotal fodder you need for your tell-all memoir.

Alright, now that we've had that huddle-up, let's get down to business. Before you throw in the towel at your 9 - 5 job, let's assess what this adventure requires. Like Rocky Balboa, if you want to go the distance, proving you're not just "another bum from the neighborhood," then you have to be sure you're ready to give it all you've got. Take it from us, you need to consider your intellectual, emotional, social, financial, and creative strengths before you put the gloves on.

Personally Speaking...

Responsibility:

Are you a self-starter who can keep to schedules, adhere to deadlines (without a manager), and answer when things go wrong? It's called *taking ownership*. When you're out on your own, there's no one to pass the buck to but yourself. So if you get careless and make a mistake, you have to take responsibility. It's *going to happen*. Even the most careful and detail-oriented people make mistakes and it's absolutely okay, we're only human.

Can you roll with the punches and quickly transition from Creative Dance Party into Problem Solving Mode? Can you set aside your personal feelings to do what's best for the business/client/fill in the blank? (It's crazy how tough a pill pride can be to swallow, especially the first few times.)

The thing is, if you take on work and can't finish it, no one else is going to. Something is going to come up, an emergency will happen, a project will take longer than you anticipate, and the list goes on. There's no middleman, no higher-ups to blame, no manager to defer to. Are you good with that?

As a freelancer or business owner, you need to learn how to be productive, how to get past creative blocks, and how to keep yourself, your team (if you have one), and your client on track even when you're tired and uninspired. You must have a sense of duty for the client. If you consistently fail to deliver timely, well-executed work within a reasonably agreed upon time frame, word gets around and you lose your greatest asset: a trustworthy and professional reputation.

A good reputation among your clients is what spreads into referrals and (hopefully) spurs repeat work. It's the best way to organically gain and keep clients. It's your salesperson who costs nothing, doesn't take sick days, and gives *you* all the benefits. Your reputation is the result of two things: your client's experience working with you plus how they perceive the final results of your project.

To be honest, your reputation is in the hands of your clients and peers. It's subjectively thrust upon you by outsiders, but you can absolutely help frame that perspective by being responsible and ethical. Of course, this doesn't mean you give in whenever there's a problem or tension arises on a project, but it does mean you put in the work to try to foresee, avoid, and remedy these problems.

A good reputation is as important—if not more important—than talent. In small business your reputation can be your best friend or your worst enemy when landing work. You want work because work brings the bucks and the bucks pay the bills (and sometimes even the frills).

Patience:

Being a freelancer will require patience with your client, yourself, and the world at large.

1. **Your Client:** In the documentary, *The Fog of War*, Robert McNamara, former Secretary of Defence during the Vietnam and Korean wars, is asked what he would have done differently looking back on it all. His number one lesson was: "empathize with your enemy." We're not saying that the client is your enemy, but some days it's going to feel that way. Humans are just big balls of emotions, and we all have our own baggage, bias, and points of reference. It's so important to take off our blinders, expanding our frame of reference to try and see how others live. Meet people where they're at so you can patiently find a way forward together. Dealing with clients is like dating. No two relationships are ever going to be the same. In other words: approach each client uniquely, with lots of mercy, and plenty of patience.

*
HOODZPAH
HOT-TAKE

A good reputation is as important— if not more important— than talent.

"If I offer you a glass of water, and bring back a cup of ice, I'm trying to teach you patience. And also that sometimes you get ice with no water, and later you'll get water with no ice. Ah, but that's life, no?"

- Jarod Kintz,
Ah, But That's
Life, No?

2. **Yourself:** Be patient with yourself! When you start working for yourself, you'll be tempted to over-promise on deadlines, deliverables, and measurable goals. You'll think you can do things faster than you actually can. You will expect to see your business grow faster than it will. Plans will fall by the wayside when you realize the time and effort it actually requires to see them through. So be patient with yourself. Don't get frustrated when you miss personal deadlines or internal goals for your business. We promise, you'll get the hang of things and become more efficient after a few years of trial and error.

3. **The World:** Patience with the world at large is the hardest of the three. You have no control over what other people will do or when they'll do it and all we can say is, leave space for lateness. Overestimate deadlines when you can to account for dropped balls and missed deadlines because of outside forces—i.e. a printer who doesn't deliver on time, a subcontractor who leaves you high-and-dry on a project, natural disasters, traffic jams, cops, random injuries, server crashes, computer problems—all things that are out of your control, but still affect your work. What you can't control must not cripple you from owning the things you can. Be honest with your clients when these things happen and let them know how you're working to lessen their impact. After all, this is life. Get used to its hang ups and a change of plans. Do your best to find gratitude for the altered path.

Organization:

It's not the glamorous side of business, but it's definitely the framework of a successful one. As a freelancer, you'll need to be able to orchestrate a project from seed to soup: getting the correct specs and goals from the client, creating and sending invoices, making contracts, logging your hours, making sure you remain on budget, meeting project benchmarks, and logging final job data for broader business review. You have to manage every aspect of your client's interaction, your project time schedule, as well as your own personal and business responsibilities (like posting to social media, updating your portfolio, etc.). Organization and planning make this work efficient.

The Gift of Research:

New freelancers and small business owners are a lot like new parents: scared and unsure. However, both seem to survive with the gift of research. You can't know everything, but you can sure look like you do if you know how to find the answers. You'll spend a lot of time troubleshooting business and project questions via Google, online forums, creative groups, mentors, and friends and family. So build your roster of expert panelists and ace resources. Remember to reward good advice with beer, handwritten thank you notes, gifts, and picking up the tab.

"The secret to multitasking is that it isn't actually multitasking. It's just extreme focus and organization."

- Joss Whedon, Director

Honesty and a Competitive Ego:

These are equally important attributes when working alone or spearheading your own business. They serve as a great check and balance for not going full wallflower nor full megalomaniac. Once you've honestly assessed whether or not you can execute a project well, you need the ego to conquer it head on. Ego keeps you competitive and sharp, it drives you to prove to your clients and peers that you are capable. It makes for great work, just don't let it keep you from constructive criticism. Trusting yourself is one thing, but being blind to the outside world, blocking out the opportunity to grow, is just plain stupid. Be humble enough to learn, it'll make your work and your work systems better. A healthy, competitive ego should actually encourage you to take the advice you need to improve.

Technically Speaking...

Know-How:

Are your design/photography/writing/creative skills ready to handle the projects that you're seeking? Make sure you're not losing efficiency and time to bad habits and jerry-rigged solutions in your programs and files. Stay on top of advancements in technology and software. Grow your skills to match ever-improving tools. Are you laying out books in Adobe Illustrator and designing logos in Photoshop? If so, then you might want to work on your program knowledge. (Owning power drills doesn't mean you know how to build a house.) One great thing about the internet age is that you don't have to go to school for four years to learn these skills, though that is certainly one way to do it. Online courses, craft-specific workshops, and trade schools can teach you what you need to know for a fraction of the cost. As always, make sure to do your research on the outfit offering your course, because paying half-rate for a shoddy education is just as maddening as paying through the nose for a decent one.

Experience:

This should be a given, but do you have the experience and portfolio you need to get work? Does your portfolio look professional while showing a marketable range? If you nab a client, do you have the work experience to effectively take them through all the stages of a new project? Experience in client interaction is essential. You need to know how to guide your client toward making the educated decisions they might not know how to get to on their own. If you are intuitively gifted at interacting with humans, that's excellent news. If you're unsure or timid, consider working for "the man" a little longer so you can learn a few more of these soft skills. Established businesses usually have systems and procedures set up, and you can learn valuable lessons about what to do, and what not to do.

Delegation:

To delegate or not to delegate? Consider whether the time and effort it'll take you to do *A* would be better spent doing *B*. Can someone else do *A* better and more efficiently than you? Does that leave you time to do something that makes your company more profitable? Do you have the funds to justify the cost? If so, then all roads lead to delegation.

Once you delegate, you have to get used to managing that delegation in a way that works for both you and your helper. Delegating is pointless if you micromanage and redo their work. Can you vet contractors, give them adequate project information, clear design direction and feedback, and keep them on track to meet your goal? Do they deliver and measure up? Delegation is an acquired skill that takes planning, organization and good communication. Even then, finding people who fit your style of doing business can take time. If after a decent trial period, the results don't justify the cost, reassess. Don't be afraid to end relationships if they aren't working. Try new players until you find the right fit, or resolve that it's easier to do it yourself for now.

Logistically Speaking...

Financials:

In your first year, you will have quite a few expenses, even if you are working from home. Before you start out on your own, you need to create a budget outlining the costs you'll need to cover and a roadmap for making a profit (we'll be doing this in an upcoming chapter). Do you have the cash? How can you minimize costs? Do you have a financial buffer so you are not betting all your money on your first year with no leeway for unexpected twists and turns? Do you have competitive rates for your proposed services? How many jobs will you need to land at those rates to be profitable? These are the questions you need to explore. Perhaps you keep your day job while you test out your freelance on the side. Or get a part-time job to supplement your freelance. There's nothing wrong with dipping your toe in freelance until you can justify the full-time leap financially.

Tools and Venue:

Do you have a computer, necessary programs, an office desk, and an ergonomic chair that won't destroy your butt and back after a day's work? Do you have the tools and skills to create your own website? In your business plan, you need to account for all these tools, whether you have them, need them, or can do without them until you start making more money. Can you work from home or will you need somewhere to work from? Account for everything. Envelopes. Accounting software. Word processing software. Giant tubs of Red Vines. Pencils. It does take money to make money in the sense of tools. Get excited: in upcoming chapters, we'll show you how to be as thrifty as possible in your first few years.

Demand:

Do you have a skill set and style that will succeed as a solo act? Are enough people seeking the kind of work/style of work you do? Is there a specific gap in the market that your skills fill? If not, then be ready to widen your net. When you start out on your own, you might have to be more of a generalist, doing work that is outside of your personal aesthetic or your preferred project type. In other words, you may have to take some less-than-glamorous jobs to pay the bills. Do you have a good enough grasp of all the programs? Can you execute a wide variety of projects? Beggars/beginners can't be choosers. Doing work you might not specialize in can keep the lights on until you have a higher demand for what you're passionate about. Of course, make sure all the work you do reflects well on your business. Branching out of your comfort zone can lead to lots of lessons and plenty of new possibilities. Just be willing to put in the extra work it takes to get a project done right. Take opportunities as they come your way—you might find a new creative skill (and revenue stream) for your company and you might even uncover a hidden talent. You'll also discover what you don't want to do, and that's *just* as crucial.

One more question…

If you can't land jobs that fit your style, can you take your creative aesthetic out of the equation and execute work that fits the client's needs? Is it possible for you to embrace their style while still making a project the best it can possibly be? Honestly, it's tough, but don't look down your nose and cringe at the mention of Comic Sans and drop shadows on text. Think of it as a chance to help them find a better alternative. When there's a client involved, there's also compromise.

Client Base:

Do people you know show interest in your talents? Starting a creative business without having any sort of buzz is dangerous. Before making the leap into working for yourself full-time, you need to put feelers out. Post your work on a personal portfolio website, share it with your friends and followers via social media. Do they respond well? Do they dig what you're doing and ask if you're available for freelance? If yes, awesome. This is the network you'll probably get your first clients from.

We'll repeat ourselves a few times on this because we believe it's the lowest-risk route to becoming a freelancer: start your freelance work on the side while you have a steady job to support you. Once client demand for your services is high enough to justify going full-time, make the move.

*

HOODZPAH HOT-TAKE

Take opportunities as they come your way—you might find a new design skill (and revenue stream) for your company and you might even uncover a hidden talent.

Boom. A treacherous leap just became an easy step. Ideally the job that supports you while you chase your freelance dreams will be in the creative field so you keep gaining experience, growing your network, and reputation.

Meet the Many Hats

As a freelancer and small business owner, you have to be able to wear many hats. Until you can expand your team, you and any partner(s) will be responsible for a lot...and it's not always the things you want. While being involved with every part of your business can be tedious, it's actually a great way to keep tabs on the overall health of your company as you grow. Trust us: the creative work will only be part of your day. You might be able to delegate some of these roles, but you should still make yourself familiar enough with them to understand their purpose.

CEO:

You have to decide the direction of your company. By looking around and ahead of you, you'll anticipate changes in the market, pivoting your approach to hedge your bets for success. Your job is to keep up on the industry, devising new ways to stay competitive. Evaluate your success and failures to better steer your company's actions.

CFO:

You have to oversee all of the company's finances. Keep your books up to date, gathering all the needed info and receipts when tax season rolls around. You're going to be intimately familiar with your financials, knowing just how much income and how many expenses you have. Are they justified? Can you cut the fat? What is the acceptance v. rejection rate on your proposals? Is there a common reason why? Should you, perhaps, consider raising or lowering your rates based on this knowledge?

Even if you delegate out the more tedious financial tasks involved in your small business, you still need to be aware of the overall profitability of your efforts so you know what decisions and changes to approve. You're the captain of this ship.

Creative:

This is the fun part. This is what we're all here for. We'll leave this bit to you.

Marketing Manager:

You have to promote your company and services in unique and effective ways. You have to manage your social media accounts, place ads as needed, create campaigns, find your target market, find new emerging markets, and so much more.

Sales Manager:

You have to woo the client, create quotes for the client, and eventually land the client.

HR Manager:

If you subcontract or hire employees, you are responsible for their happiness, engagement, and making sure everyone— including you—is treated fairly.

Administrator:

You have to deal with all the emails, scheduling, organization, and file management that keep your projects (and company) running smoothly. You might get an assistant for the more mundane facets of admin, but you're still the grand overseer of all communication as it relates to you and your company. It all reflects on you, ultimately.

As you can see, running your own company takes an investment of time and effort. Start small with the time that you have, and see if it's for you. A few good projects make all this work worth while. You'll see. The freelance bug strikes without warning. We got hooked quick. And soon, working for someone else felt so much less fulfilling than the excitement of running our own gig.

Don't worry. This page is intentionally blank in case you want to tear out the poster on the next page.

Illustration by Amy Hood of Hoodzpah (Hoodzpahdesign.com)

2

Get by With a Little Help

Even a solo act needs a backup band.

———

Assemble Your A-Team

No man is an island. In fact, we're a lot more like Hobo Stew: the joint effort of all the people who offered knowledge and insight over the years. Whether you're starting out on your own, or you've got a crew of partners, you're going to need help from some (or all) of the people below. To be honest, you might not retain their services after your initial set-up or consultation, but it's really helpful to utilize their skills at the beginning of your business.

Ignorance is not bliss in business. Get used to advice and constructive criticism from people in your industry as well as outsiders (they usually have a beneficially unique perspective). Our own business mentor isn't in a creative field at all. The feedback you get won't always be easy to hear, especially when it points out your own user error; But the ability to take and utilize differing opinions and advice is crucial. It keeps you relevant and adaptable. You don't have to take every note you're given, but considering things from other perspectives will absolutely stress-test your concept in a way you couldn't do alone. It almost always results in a better product, process, or service.

Trial by Fire is more than a Journey comeback album (one with a hilarious cover image—imagine a souvenir t-shirt airbrush artist trying to emulate the surreal style of a Pink Floyd album cover). It's also how we can refine an idea. With the help of the following people, you'll make sure you're making decisions for your business that are smart and won't put you at risk.

A Bank:

When you start a new business, you need to setup a business account that is separate from your personal account. Most people set it up with the same bank they use for their personal finances, but you can shop around. Consider rates, services offered, and the bank's ability to work with the U.S. Small Business Administration's loan system. Most importantly: is the banker you meet with aware of the needs of a small business? Are they invested in helping you navigate murky banking waters? You need to feel comfortable talking with them and asking them questions.

Having a separate account for your business isn't required by law, but it makes bookkeeping and general accounting a lot easier. Like, A LOT. If you have to comb through your account every month to separate personal and business, you're self-inflicting unnecessary pain. Spare your sanity and save your time by keeping them separate. Have a card exclusively for business expenses and be diligent about not using it for personal expenses. It's easier and keeps things above-board. Also, if you're looking to grow into partners and employees, this is a best practice to start from the beginning.

New business checking accounts are often free to open as long as you keep to the minimum required balance. Check with your bank of choice to know the options and fees associated with having various accounts so you can make sure you're maximizing your deal. After all, it's your money and they want it.

Paperwork. There is some paperwork required for setting up a business account. The documents vary depending on your business structure (we'll get into this later), but have a conversation with your banker. They want to help you out and keep you happy. Know that if you're doing business under a name other than your legal name, you do need to file a DBA (Doing Business As) or Fictitious Name Certificate before you can open a bank account. Don't worry, we'll cover this acronym more in upcoming chapters.

A Business Mentor:

This is someone you know and trust who can offer you guidance. Usually this is a person who is already in your life and they're already guiding you without knowing you consider them a mentor. You can also ask someone to be your mentor. Your mentor might be in your industry, or they might just be a generally business savvy individual. Ideally they've been around the block (in a strictly business sense); they know the ropes, and they have both the patience and wisdom to help you avoid mistakes.

A good mentor can be one of the most important people in your business life. Take advantage of the fact that they've walked this road—or a similar road—before you, and are willing to let you learn from the blood, sweat and tears they've shed. You'll more than likely have a few different mentors throughout the course of your business. As your understanding evolves, you'll attract and be attracted to different people who can help you grow. The key is to find someone who has the time, experience and interest in helping you. Never take them for granted. It's an unbelievable gift they're offering.

A mentorship is usually unpaid and informal but make your mentor feel appreciated for everything they do. If they help you make an important decision or if they take the time to give you advice, be sure to show your gratitude in both word and deed. Buy lunch, send a handwritten note (never goes out of style) or a personalized gift. If they refer you work, definitely give them a referral fee (percentage of the project landed). You never want these business guardian angels to feel taken for granted. They don't owe you anything.

Also, don't take advantage. It's one thing to ask for an opinion, it's another to ask them for the play-by-play game plan of how to run your company. If you need more than a quick opinion, ask about paying them for an hour or two of specific consultation. It's important to be sensitive and respectful of boundaries and proprietary information. They might only be allowed to tell you so much, they also might be in a competing industry.

*

HOODZPAH
HOT-TAKE

RE: ASKING FOR ADVICE

Don't take advantage. It's one thing to ask for an opinion, it's another to ask them for the play-by-play game plan of how they run their company.

If you're both designers (or photographers/writers/etc.) don't ask them what they charge for the services you both offer. Depending on the level of your relationship, they might freely offer it up, but asking for it almost always feels invasive. If you're curious how your rates compare or if you're over / under charging, tell them what you're charging (or planning to charge) and ask for feedback. That's a less presumptuous way to get the ball rolling. Remember: they're a resource, they aren't here to do the work for you.

There's a saying, "I love you like a son, but I didn't take you to raise," and that's often the case. Be respectful and don't cross boundaries. Your mentor has put in a lot of work. It's not fair to make them into your cheat sheet to a quick paycheck. Do your own homework and try to come up with your own strategy. Take that to them with your questions and notes. This shows them you are willing to work, and that you value their time.

A CPA (Certified Public Accountant):

Your CPA is your business' Samwise Gamgee. They help you find your way when you're caught in the sticky web of financial inarticulacy and you can't get out. Note that there are accountants and there are CPAs. Business coach Jean Murray explains the difference: "Accountants do the routine work and they can complete tax returns, while CPAs can analyze the work, represent you at a tax audit, and help you make more high-level business and tax decisions. Sure, CPAs charge more, but you get what you pay for." If you get just one individual to help you, get a CPA. If you use a firm, find one that has CPAs and accountants so you might pay less for routine work, but you'll have the option for analysis as needed.

Traits to look for in your CPA: Patience in spades, doesn't mind taking the time to explain things to you, will help you weigh pros and cons of your financial decisions, and can speak your language when it comes to taxes, planning and the like. Try www.SmallBizAccountants.com.

When you first start your business, be sure to have an accountant help you set up your tax payment schedule (getting this wrong could result in missed payments, piles of fees, and a few "oh, crikey" moments). Your accountant can also help file all your taxes and, eventually, they may even manage your monthly bookkeeping and payroll.

Good design begins with honesty, asks tough questions, comes from collaboration and from trusting your intuition.

- Freeman Thomas, Automobile Designer

When we started Hoodzpah, we only needed an accountant to file our quarterly taxes and to prepare our annual taxes. We did our own monthly bookkeeping with Quickbooks, eventually switching to Xero.

A Lawyer:

Find a lawyer, preferably one who specializes in Small Business Law. Bring them your business plan and start asking questions. Get their advice because, chances are, they've seen a lot of people do what you're about to attempt, and they may save you some grief.

Things to get their word on: Precautions to consider when conducting business, contracts (writing, upholding, modifying standard contracts, etc.), structuring your business (will you be a sole proprietor, a partnership, corporation, LLC., etc.).

If you don't have the money for a lawyer, look to friends or family who are lawyers. Offer to take them to lunch and be prepared with specific, direct questions. Offer a trade: your creative skills for their legal expertise. Don't be awkward about it, though—be direct, respectful and clear about the parameters and scope of the trade. And be OK if they say no.

An Insurance Agent:

Even if you work from home, talking to an insurance agent is a smart move. In fact, talk to a few. Consider online options like Freelancers Union. There are a lot of bases to cover. Insurances can include (but are not limited to):

a. **Personal Health Insurance:** Many people get their health insurance (and their family's) through their employer. If you are now your sole employer, it falls to you to provide this.

b. **Disability Insurance:** If you get hurt or become seriously ill and cannot work, this kind of coverage can generally replace around 60 percent of your income.

c. **Life Insurance**: If you die, this insurance will pay out a lump-sum to your beneficiaries. The idea is that you won't leave loved ones without provision, in the event of your death. It's also one of the main reasons Forensic Files has 406 episodes across 15 seasons.

d. **Business Insurance:** The breadth of this insurance depends on your situation. It could include property insurance (homeowner's insurance doesn't always include business property and equipment), business interruption insurance, and general liability insurance.

e. **Indemnity Insurance ("Errors and Omissions Insurance"), or Professional Liability Insurance:** This protects you from being sued by clients who claim your negligence caused an error or omission in the product you made for them. Whether you're right or wrong in the incident, legal fees associated with fighting a lawsuit could be crippling to your business. Some client contracts will require you carry this insurance. As an extra measure for this type of risk, ask your lawyer if they can add a clause into your contract to limit your liability on projects.

---

*

HOODZPAH HOT-TAKE

RE: BARTERING SERVICES

Don't be awkward about it— be direct, respectful and clear about the parameters and scope of the trade.

Freelance, and Business, and Stuff: A Guide for Creatives

You will be pitched to buy every kind of insurance out there. But prioritize "must have" insurance against what you can go without. As your company grows and your liability grows, you'll need to adjust your insurance coverage to suit. The bigger the projects, the bigger the payouts, the bigger the liability. Weigh pros and costs and pick wisely.

Remember that you aren't required to have every insurance. Also remember that you're human, and honest mistakes can still lead to lawsuits from unhappy or harmed clients. Some insurance is required. Health care under the U.S.'s Affordable Care Act is required as of the date of this book being published. If you forgo enrolling, you'll have to pay an IRS tax penalty.

Chapter Checklist: To Do

- [ ] Get a business bank account.
- [ ] Gather your A-Team of Advisors and Professional Consultants.
- [ ] Inquire about insurance.

CA$H RULES EVERY THING AROUND ME

Illustration by Amy Hood of Hoodzpah (Hoodzpahdesign.com)

3

Making a Budget

"Cash rules everything around me."
- Wu-Tang Clan

Let's start this chapter with a vow to have fun with it. Let's rename it *Financial Funsies*. Why? Because, for the most part, money is fun and awesome. It pays for your everyday needs, your food, your shelter. It will pay for your health care, your son's baking classes, your daughter's birthday bounce house, and your live-in adult brother's expensive and morally questionable Pay-Per-View habit. It also pays for the faux Eames chairs you'll undoubtedly buy for your office (a fur throw draped on it = +10 Instagram likes). Money puts overpriced lattes in your hand, and ensures that your Netflix addiction proceeds without interruption.

For all these reasons and more, making more money rather than less of it is rad, right? That means you can pay off your student loans, save up for a vacation, plus lay away cash for your retirement in Palm Springs (can you see the 60+ community populated by velour track suits and Bob-Barker-level tans?). Let's start making plans for this. As we're tallying the numbers and crunching the data, just keep envisioning what you'll buy with your extra income. Is your carrot affixed to the end of your stick? Then let's giddy up.

Defining Our Terms

Budget: an estimate of the money you make versus the money you spend and/or save for a set period of time.

Income or Revenue: money you earn for your services, products, and investments.

Net Income or Profit: a business's total income minus what it spends in expenses (like taxes, supplies, payroll, equipment, etc.).

Expense: money spent to conduct your business. Examples of expenses could include paying for the coffee you have when meeting with a client, paying for a stock photo, or paying for your Adobe Creative Cloud subscription.

Profit / Loss Statement: also called an income statement, this is a financial statement that totals the money coming into your business (revenue) versus money going out (expenses and costs) during a specific period of time. The difference between a profit/loss statement and a budget is that a budget is a goal for future income and expenses over a period of time, and a profit/loss looks back on the actual income and expenses over a period of time.

The Almighty B Word: Budgeting

Congress gives budgets a bad reputation. Budgets might seem convoluted and anxiety-riddled. But they're not. They're easy when you don't have to get the approval of 535 people to pass them. In this case, it's just you (and your business partners if you have them). A budget gives you a reference point to base your income and pricing. Knowing your budget means you know how much you can spend and how much you need to make to reach your financial goals.

In this chapter, we'll start by making a personal budget. This sheds light on what you need to personally make. Then, we'll make a business budget. This paints a picture of what your company needs to make in income to cover your wages, the cost of doing business, and the savings/re-investment plan you'll set up.

Think of your budget like a financial food pyramid. There are certain food groups that need to be met in certain quantities to stay healthy. Our financial food pyramid is made up of three groups: needs, wants, and savings.

For your personal budget worksheet, we'll use a simple guideline created by Senator Elizabeth Warren and her daughter Amelia Warren Tyagi in their book, *All Your Worth: The Ultimate Lifetime Money Plan*. They call it the 50-30-20 Budget. You take your after-tax income and plan to use 50% of it for your needs, 30% for your wants, and 20% for savings. It's a very friendly system that can hardly be called austere. This is a budget that won't make you suffer in joyless scrimping (blow-up mattress + Cup Noodles every meal = sad face), and will put you on track to pay off debts and build savings.

For your business budget worksheet, we'll calculate your overall expenses to do business (including taxes), and anything on top of that will be for savings and re-investment. To give you a reference, at Hoodzpah, our goal for business savings in the beginning was to get two months worth of operating expenses stowed away in the bank (meaning, we could run our business as usual and pay our wages without any new work coming in for two months). That way we had a safety buffer for slow months. Eventually our savings and re-investment plan grew.

Now, get your pencils and pens ready, we're going to dive into the budget worksheets!

》》》

Important Disclaimer: This chapter is based on our own personal experience. Review this plan with your CPA or financial advisor to make sure it's a good fit for you. This is not a substitute for legal and other professional advice where the facts and circumstances warrant.

Make a Personal Budget

We're going to start your Personal Budget by calculating your needs **per month** below. Exclude savings. Exclude wants (meaning, leave out anything non-essential like designer clothes, expensive coffee / cocktails, eating out, and so on). It'll be hard to separate some needs and wants, but just do your best. As far as loans and debts, only include minimum required payments in this section. Exclude business expenses for now. This is only for personal needs. Fill in the blanks next to each item in the sections below. Add in any expenses that are unique to you, which we might not have a section for. Add section totals together for total monthly "Needs" sum. If you provide for more people than just yourself, consider the total money needed for you and your dependants.

My Essential Needs per Month

Loans/Debt

Min. Credit Card Payment

Min. Student Loan Payment

Other Min. Payments

Home/Utilities:

Mortgage/Rent/HOA

Gas/Oil

Electricity

Water and Sewer

Maintenance

Phone

Cable/Internet

Security

Personal Care

Personal Hygiene Needs

Clothes/Apparel

Prescriptions

Out-of-Pocket Medical

Insurance

Life

Auto

Home

Health

Auto

Min. Car Loan/Lease

Car Maintenance

Public Transit

Parking

Gas

Dependants

Pet Supplies

Veterinary Costs

Child/Elderly Care

Child Support

Groceries

Total Needs per Month:

Now that you've figured out your monthly needs number, multiply it by 12 to get your yearly number. From here we're going to work backwards to get our Total Budget amount. Remember the 50-30-20 Budget breakdown: 50% is for needs, 30% for wants, and 20% for savings. So if we know that needs makes up half of our total budget, we can multiply our yearly needs by two to get our total yearly budget. Then calculate what 30% of your total budget is to find your "wants" allowance, and 20% of your total budget for your "savings" allowance. Do the math below to find your totals.

Needs/month x 12 = Yearly Needs

Yearly Needs x 2 = Total Yearly Budget

You'll need this number on the next page!

Total Yearly Budget x 0.3 = Yearly Wants

Total Yearly Budget x 0.2 = Yearly Savings

Example:

If your yearly needs totalled $30,000, then based on the 50-30-20 budget, your Yearly Total Budget is twice that, or $60,000.
$60,000 x 0.3 = $18,000 of your Yearly Budget allotted for wants per year (like a weekend in Big Sur and tickets to *Hamilton*).
$60,000 yearly budget x 0.2 = $12,000 in savings (rainy day fund, college fund, unexpected illness fund, paying off debts early fund, retirement fund, etc.).

Calculate Estimated Yearly Personal Income Goal (Before Taxes)

Your total Yearly Personal Budget represents what you need to make in take-home pay, but it doesn't account for taxes (state, federal and otherwise). So now we need to calculate estimated total taxes and add that on top* to get your Yearly Personal Income goal "Before Taxes", meaning before taxes are taken out. If you don't save extra for these taxes, then you'll have to pay for them out of your take-home pay, which cuts into your wants and savings. When you were employed by someone else, they paid these taxes for you. But now you have to pay your own taxes on income you earn working for yourself.

In the United States, depending on how much money you make, where you live, and your tax filing status, your total tax rate could be between 20-35% of your income (ask your CPA). If you're planning on making $400,000+ personally (we can dream), then prepare yourself for closer to a 40% tax rate in the United States. Save more rather than less when it comes to taxes, so you'll have a safe buffer. Extra savings at the end of the year isn't a bad thing. For those of you living in other countries, check with your accountant about your tax rate. In the below equation, we're figuring out what 30% of your total yearly budget is, to save that for taxes. To use another tax rate in the below equation, move the decimal point of the tax rate to the left two places and use that number instead of 0.3 (example: for a 20% tax rate, use 0.2 in the below equation, instead of 0.3).

Total Yearly Budget x 0.3 = Estimated Yearly Taxes

Yearly Taxes + Total Yearly Budget = Estimated Yearly Personal Income (Before Taxes)*

Example:

Using the example Yearly Total Budget from the previous page, $60,000:
60,000 x .3 = $18,000 in Yearly Taxes. Add that back on top of the $60,000, and you get an estimated Yearly Personal Income goal (Before Taxes) of $78,000.

This equation isn't an exact method, since 30% of your income before taxes wont be the same as 30% of your income after taxes (it's a bit brain fry-ing). But this simple equation is good for a rough approximation. To factor in your deductions and get a more exact number for your yearly taxes, try an online tax calculator like: www.smartasset.com/taxes/income-taxes Thanks to Ethan Young Unzicker, a reader who sent in thoughts and suggestions that made this section better!

Now we know what your desired yearly income is! This is your optimal estimation. But in order to justify it, you'll have to bring in the work at the right price to support it. The 50-30-20 Budget is not for everyone, and as you make more you may alter the percentages. Adjust the numbers to suit your unique needs. The most important thing is that you find a way to meet your budget income goals by making enough money in your freelancing endeavours. Budgeting is not a one-time thing. You are constantly adjusting and tweaking your budget and your desired income based on changing life situations, changing business seasons (some months are good, some months are slow) and changing economic times. In our pricing chapter, we'll help you plan out your income sources so you hopefully reach your goal.

As you do business, it will be important to look at your company's profit/loss statement each month to see if you're on track with the amount of needed income to support your budget. If you're not bringing in enough money, you'll have to scale back on wants and tighten your purse strings, or find some side work to make up the difference. Running your own business means you have to stay on top of things so your finances don't run away unchecked. Monthly fluctuation is normal, but beware longer downward trends. Spending more than you make leads to financial and emotional disaster. Once you build up savings, the very normal ebb and flow of work becomes less stressful. Your backup cash will cover your months of famine until the months of feast come back. If you have two or three bad months in a row, start to look at your pricing, service offering, and method of doing business. Something might need to be adjusted. The definition of insanity is doing the same thing over and over, expecting different results. Maybe the market has changed. Maybe your client base has changed. Maybe you're not communicating the value of your services to potential clients.

Check Your Calculations Against Real Industry Averages

After doing this budget and income exercise, see how your desired income stacks up against employed creatives across the United States. Check out The Creative Group's yearly resource called the "Salary Forecast" (at the time of writing this, you can get this forecast free if you subscribe to their parent company newsletter at www.RobertHalf.com). In it, they list average salary ranges for the most common

---

*

HOODZPAH HOT-TAKE

RE: SLOW MONTHS

If you have two or three slow months in a row, you need to rethink things. You might be overvaluing what others are willing to pay for your work. But more than likely, you just need to better prove the value of your pricing to clients.

creative positions. The list shows variation depending on experience level and location in the United States. You can request a copy or get one free on their website by signing up for their email newsletter. By comparing your budget income goal with the industry average, you can see if you're competitive, shooting high, or below the national average. You don't have to adjust your number to match the average. If your work is more highly sought after, and your style of work is rare, you can charge more. There are tons of factors that go into what your salary can be. The goal here is to get a sense of where your number sits in the industry landscape.

Now that we've worked out what you need to make personally in take-home pay, we're going to calculate your business budget. This budget can be simpler. We won't use the 50-30-20 Budget here. Rather, we'll just tally your business expenses. Your business budget needs to include your desired yearly income (before taxes are taken out) as well as any other estimated costs of doing business (equipment, subcontractors, software, etc.). Any income you make above these total business expenses is your profit margin. You can save this money and/or choose to re-invest it. Talk to your financial advisor or CPA to figure out a plan that works for you.

>>>

Make a Business Budget

Now let's plan your business budget. Think of all your estimated expenses (what you have to spend to run your business). **Calculate these per year**, as there are a lot of one-time yearly costs for a business.

My Business Expenses per Year

Office

Rent/Lease/Mortgage

Postage/Shipping

Supplies

Maintenance

Phone & Internet

Utilities

Software/Hardware

Subscriptions

Furniture

Loans/Debt

Credit Card

Business Loan

Food & Gifts

Business / Meeting-Related Meals

Promotional Gifts

Marketing

Advertising

Website

Etc. Collateral

Travel for Business

Company Car

Public Transit

Parking

Gas

Flying

Hotels

Personnel

Cost of My Salary (before taxes)

Other Employee Salaries

Subcontractors

Lawyer

Accountant

Etc.

Business Licenses

Business Insurance

Business Taxes
Ask your CPA what to save for your business taxes, as it varies widely depending on your business structure and income.

Total Business Expenses per Year:

Business Expenses per Year + Business Savings Goal per Year = Total Yearly Business Budget

Congrats, you business savvy numbers wizard! You've figured out your business expenses and total budget. Now your aim is to bring in enough work to meet this budget goal. Are you looking at these numbers and feeling overwhelmed as to how you'll make enough money to cover it? Fret not. Remember that budgets are goals, not required benchmarks. Budgets are living documents that you can adjust and adapt as you go. If you start doing business and realize you won't be able to meet the budget goal, find ways to trim down your expenses. How? Glad you asked. Here are some ways to drastically reduce your cost of doing business.

Expense Hacks

Embrace Working from Home

This is the best possible scenario to cut your costs as long as you can remain productive and focused at home. Your first few years of freelancing will be stressful enough as you try and gain new clients and bring in work. So keep your overhead as low as possible to lessen your financial burden while you iron out the kinks in your process and income streams. There's less risk and it's more convenient. Can you imagine signing a year lease on an office and then losing your main client two months later? *Quelle nightmare*! Just carve out your own home office space that's quiet and cosy.

Working from home has its perks, too. You work when you need to and take breaks when you want to. If you had an office open to the public, you'd have to keep regular office hours and deal with the occasional walk-in asking you to design business cards for their doggy makeover company. You'd have to deal with traffic like the rest of the rat race. Working from home means no commute less car expenses as a result. Hoodzpah is a remote office, and we choose to work from a home office to this day, because we prefer the convenience and flexibility.

If you decide to work from home, set boundaries with roommates and/or family members so they respect your work area and don't distract you. Routine and structure will still be key to staying on task and getting work done. Try and find a daily routine that works best for you. Winging it and waiting till you feel "inspired" every day won't cut it. Freelance freedom is easily abused, and can spiral into a de-motivated nightmare. Some days you'll battle the boredom of flying solo. You'll need creative feedback. You'll crave social interaction from someone besides your cat. That's why it's hugely important to stay plugged into the creative community, online and offline. Find creative friends who don't

*

HOODZPAH HOT-TAKE

RE: WORKING FROM HOME

Make a pact to ignore your computer during set off-hours.

mind you sending them progress shots of your work through email or Slack. Most of them have probably been looking for a friend to send their work to as well.

Most of all, when working from home, remember that your home isn't an office 24/7. Make a pact to ignore your computer during set off-hours. Once work is over, your personal time is for friends, family, and just plain loafing around. Your business might be in your home, but you can't let it dictate your life all the time. Be thoughtful of segmenting the two. It will preserve your sanity.

Co-Working Spaces

If you have to get office space, be realistic about cost and do the math to figure out what you can afford. If you can't afford your own office, look into co-working spaces. Collaborative work space co-ops are popping up everywhere, offering reasonable rates for shared spaces with like-minded folk. You can rent a desk for a day (if you have a big meeting), or get a desk for a few days a week. It's cheaper than paying for your own office, and it gives you the community/work/life balance you need.

Working Remote

If you can't afford an office or co-working space, but you get distracted or depressed working at home, try changing your scenery. Grab your laptop and head to a place with free Wi-Fi—the library, a coffee shop, a restaurant, and even a bar can all be your office-away-from-home. Bring headphones if you need more quiet. If you don't have all your programs on your laptop, then use this remote work time to do logo sketches, prepare quotes and proposals, or write up a blog post on a recent project. You'll remain productive while stimulating your senses and curing your cabin fever. Who knows, maybe you'll meet your next client while out and about. If you want to work in an office environment, reach out to friends who have office spaces for their own businesses. They might have an extra desk or room where you can hang out and work for the day. Perhaps you could offer them a certain amount of services per month in exchange for a regular desk to work at.

Curb the Itch to Upgrade

When you land that big project, or get that first big freelance check, it's going to be tempting to spend it. But here's the thing, if you spend more money as you make more money, then you're not really making more money. The biggest trap of new wealth is to live to your means, rather than live to your needs. We see it with new actors or athletes all the time. They get drafted, they get the big part, and they start spending like they'll always be making that kind of money. Then a lull happens in their career, or an injury strikes, and they wind up bankrupt. They weren't saving, and they let their expenses grow to fill their income. As your income grows, try to keep your expenses low. You can treat yourself, of course, but don't let your expenses grow to match your income. You can never save money this way.

As a new professional you'll be tempted to upgrade your car, your closet, your equipment. Unless you have good cash flow and savings to justify it, put these upgrades off and make do with less. If you have an old car, and you're worried big clients won't take you seriously if they see you drive up in it, then take a car service to your meeting. A few Lyfts is better than the burden of a new car loan. If you have an older iPhone, you don't have to upgrade just because everyone else is. A slightly older computer or laptop won't kill you. If it can handle the programs and processes you need it for, then don't upgrade. If you have a good shared rent situation with someone, you don't have to move out into your own place yet. Just because you're an entrepreneur doesn't mean you have to 2.0 your life. Keep things as they are for the first year of freelance, if you can. Then look at your year, the trends, and what you've saved, and see where you can re-invest (new equipment, etc.) or treat yourself.

There can be a lot of pressure in creative industries to look a certain part and have certain toys. But you know what's cooler? Not having to stress about making a car payment when you're starting a new business. Not having to take crap jobs just to make rent. Not getting ulcers from stress about work. Make a habit of curbing your spending impulses. This talent will serve you well in famine years. The economy won't always be awesome. Bad stretches will happen, and you won't get a heads up on when they'll hit. Low expenses and a fat savings will make these dips in the market easier to survive.

Budgeting for Freedom and Flexibility

For both your business and personal budgets, your goal is to make more than you spend. Eliminate your credit and loan debts as soon as possible, and start your "F*** You Fund." There's an article by Michael Korda for *The New Yorker* where he profiles Irving Lazar, a famous talent agent who represented the likes of Humphrey Bogart, Truman Capote, Faye Dunaway and more. Lazar tells him, "The first million bucks you make—put it away! You don't ever touch that, you hear me? That's your 'F*** you' money. That way, anybody ever tries to make you do something you don't want to do, you can tell 'em, 'F*** you.'" Some iteration of this proverb is echoed across books and memoirs by all kinds of authors. Your number might be different than the million Lazar recommends (ours sure was). But the point is, it's easier to choose your path when you have the financial freedom to say "no". Building up savings gives you the confidence to be more selective in who you work with, what you work on, and how.

Chapter Checklist: To Do

- ☐ Make a personal budget.
- ☐ Calculate your desired yearly income.
- ☐ Make a business budget.

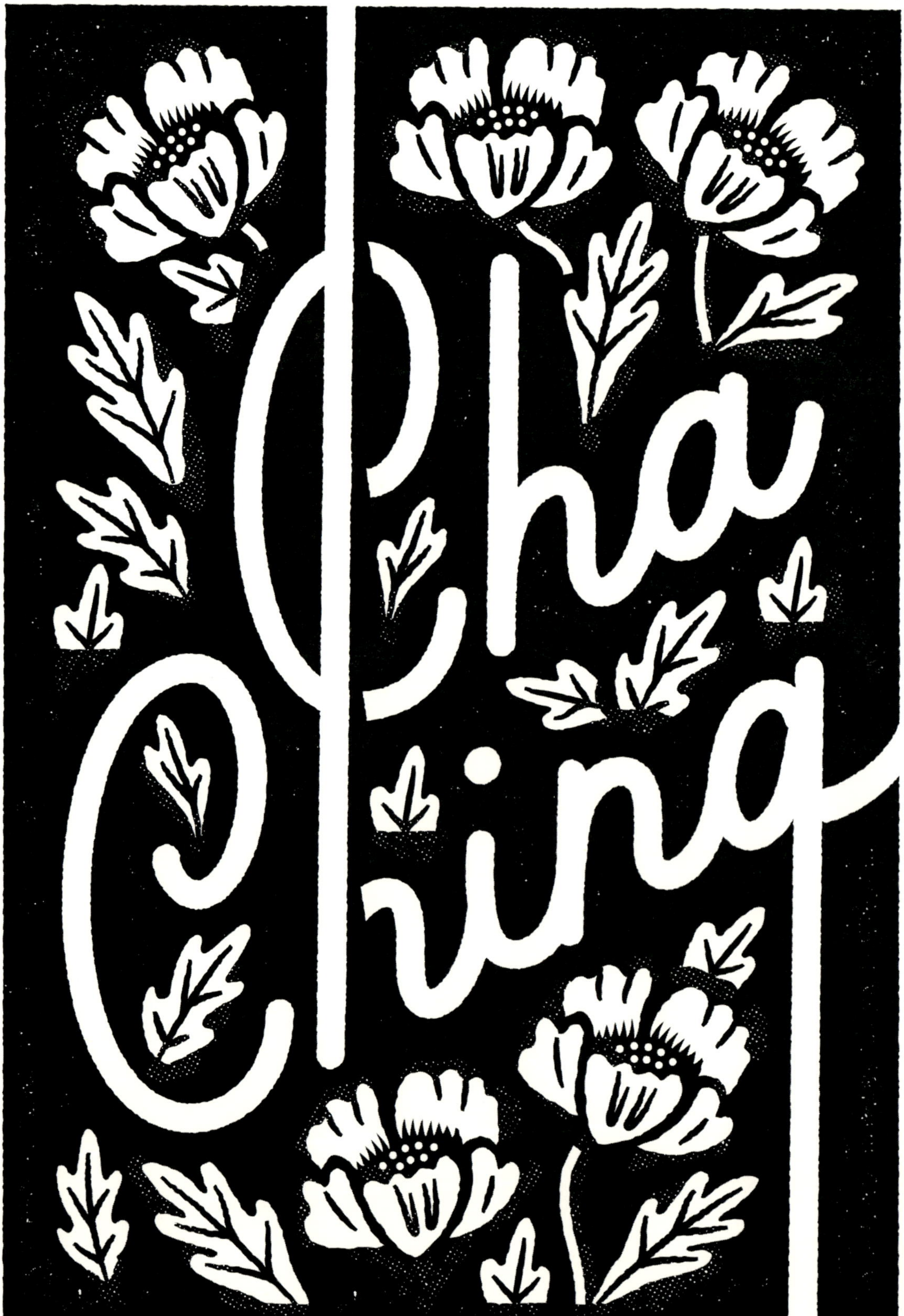

Illustration by Amy Hood of Hoodzpah (Hoodzpahdesign.com)

4
Pricing and Proposals

Value isn't inherent, it's proven.

———

There's nothing worse than someone asking you what your rate is and you derp-derping your way into a price that then sounds completely made-up. Know your rates and be confident when presenting them to a potential client. If you seem unsure and apologetic, they'll smell fear and devour you like the soft marshmallow you are.

As far as what to charge: that's the big, mysterious question to which there are an infinite number of right answers. Your pricing (flat or hourly) depends on a lot of things, not just the cost of doing business. Your pricing should reflect your experience, the demand for your work, the level of skill required for your work, the value of the project to the client, the extent to which final deliverables will be used, and other factors unique to the project.

Flat Rate vs. Hourly

There are two main types of pricing for creative fields. Each has its unique place, depending on the type of client and the type of work. Some creative jobs are best billed at a flat rate and others are better dealt with at an hourly rate. In our experience, here's how we decide which to use when:

Bill Flat Rate For:

Jobs you can quantify the scope of. You should know exactly what work, materials, and deliverables are required so you don't come up short. We like to bill flat rate for the projects we do most often since we know exactly what goes into it. Examples of these:

   a. **Logos:** If you know you will only give the client 3 concepts, 2 rounds of revisions, then save the final files for them (or whatever your process looks like), then there's a specific window you can quote for.

   b. **Spot Illustrations:** Based on the client, illustration style, and usage scenario (licensing or full buy out), you can quote accordingly.

   c. **A Photography Session:** If you know how many scenes you'll shoot, how many hours you're accounting for, how many shots you'll edit and deliver, how many revisions you'll give the client, and what licensing rights you'll allow, then you can calculate a good flat rate.

   d. **Discovery Phase:** If a project is too big to be quoted without extensive research, then flat rate a discovery phase, at the end of which you have a game plan and proposed quote for the full project. This is good for projects where clients need help figuring out their goals and deliverables.

e. **Production Work that has Clear Parameters and Deliverables:** For example, if you are laying out yet another pitch deck or catalog and you know roughly how long it takes to design per page, it might be worth creating a set price. It also gives your client the comfort of knowing exactly what the final invoice will be.

Pros of Flat Rate: The client knows exactly what they're in for and so do you. The client doesn't have to worry about the bill turning into a runaway train, and you know what scope you have to work within to make a profit. If you finish the project early, you still get paid the full amount.

Flat rate is also a great way to educate your clients about the value of your services in a way that hourly may not. Hourly doesn't account for the value of the service, it only accounts for the time spent on services rendered and the cost of resources used (photography rental equipment, etc.). For example, the logo is a core visual representation of a company. It is what that company will be recognized by for years to come. Value and equity accrue every year that the logo is used within a positive brand experience. Its value is often hard to measure. McDonald's golden arches, Coca Cola's iconic script, Nike's famous swoosh—they're worth so much more than just the hours spent in designing them. Why? Because they are intended to become the core reference point of a brand or company (at least this is our hope for any logo we work on). Therefore, you have to measure the existing and potential value of the project to the company to properly quote a logo job. This value needs to be added on top of the estimated hours you'll need to execute the work. The total is your flat rate quote.

Cons of Flat Rate: If you haven't defined the project scope clearly enough, scope creep can occur. This means you're working more than you planned for and you still have to deliver for the price upon which you and your client agreed. Alternatively, you can re-approach the client to see if you can negotiate more money (neither are optimal scenarios). This is often referred to as a Change Order or a Change Order Request.

Bill Hourly For:

a. **Jobs Where the Scope is Vague or Flexible:** You might set two hourly rates, one for production work and a higher one for creative work. This way you still build in added value beyond your exact services rendered, without quoting flat rate.

b. **Production Work with a Less Defined Scope:** Production work is not hugely creative. It's work that already has a style guide

*

HOODZPAH HOT-TAKE

Tracking hours (even when doing flat rate projects) will help you refine your flat rate pricing by staying on top of how long it actually takes you to do things on average.

or template defined, and you're just carrying out that set style and theme across more assets, or making edits to existing work. For this reason, it's easy to apply an hourly rate with no consideration of added price value for creating new designs or campaigns from scratch.

Pros of Hourly: You get paid for every hour of work you do. There's no going over budget here. It's accurate, and nixes the need to write up detailed estimates (like in flat rate quoting). You invoice based on 20/20 hindsight. We usually tell clients that we invoice in 15 minute increments, but many creatives round into hour increments to make it worthwhile as it encourages clients to use your time wisely, gathering their revisions into one cohesive bundle. Another thing to consider is implementing a minimum invoice fee. This would be the minimum hours that must be billed on an invoice. Let's say your minimum billable invoice fee is 1 hour. If someone comes to you with a small job that only takes 15 minutes, you'll still bill them for a minimum of 1 hour.

Cons of Hourly: Your client might get shocked when they get the final invoice. This is why it's important to give them updates of your time throughout the project. Hourly work invoices should never be a bad surprise. Give your client a loose estimate of how long you expect a project to take (a ballpark is fine - i.e. $xxx - $xxxx). You don't have to itemize it and explain it like a flat rate quote. Let the client know at the beginning that the estimate of hours is just that, an estimate, and that it is likely to fluctuate, but you will keep them updated. Updates might also encourage your client to be efficient and decisive on their part. Invoice regularly to avoid sticker shock (every two weeks, or at clear benchmarks in the project). If the client knows they have to pay you for every hour worked, they might try and rush you to make sure they pay less. This doesn't help the creative process and will annoy you in general. Remind them that good work doesn't always come quickly.

Sometimes one project requires both a flat rate and an hourly rate. As an example, at Hoodzpah we charge a flat rate for logo packages. If more time or revision rounds are needed above what we included in our flat rate package (3 initial concepts, 2 rounds of revisions), we stipulate in our contract that work can continue at our hourly creative rate.

Knowing when you should bill a project flat rate versus hourly, and how to accurately quote flat rate jobs, becomes easier as you gain experience. Tracking hours (even when doing flat rate projects) will help you build and refine your flat rate pricing by staying on top of how long it actually takes you to do things on average.

*

HOODZPAH
HOT-TAKE

Clients should never be shocked by their invoice. Send regular updates on hours.

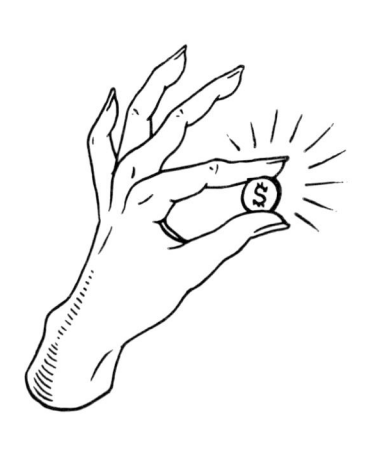

How to Calculate Your Hourly Rate

Step 1: Write down how much money you're trying to make from freelance in a year.

Step 2: Estimate your billable hours in a year.

"Billable hours" are hours worked that you can bill your clients for. These are hours directly spent on client work. Non-billable hours are spent managing your own business, and taking care of your own thankless duties (not to mention the occasional Instagram mental vacation or Pinterest binge). Estimate your billable hours for a week (Average your billable hours for several previous weeks and months of freelancing (to do this start keeping track of your hours if you aren't already), or by estimating based on your average workload. If you're freelancing full-time, your billable hours for a week in which you work 50 hours might only be 35 hours. 35 Hours spent on work that you can bill a client for, and 15 hours spent on management and building your own company. If you're working part-time the numbers will be lower. Now, to figure out your yearly billable hours, multiply your weekly billable hours by the number of weeks you'll work in a year. There are 52 weeks in a year, but you shouldn't be working all of them. You're not a robot (yet), just flesh and blood. You'll require a few weeks of rest and relaxation scattered across the year. Take it all at once, or take it here and there, just take it for your sanity and creative restoration. If you plan for two weeks' vacation, and two weeks for the unexpected things that keep you from working across a year (emergencies, sickness, etc.), then you only have 48 work weeks in a year.

Weekly Billable Hours x 48 Work weeks per Year = Billable Hours per Year (BHY)

Step 3: Find your baseline hourly rate:

Freelance Income Goal for the Year ÷ Billable Hours per Year = Baseline Hourly Rate

Example: If your goal is to make $80,000 in a year from freelance, then $80,000 divided by 1,680 BHY = $47.61 per hour

We call this your baseline hourly, because this is a starting point. Now you'll want to adjust your rate depending on your skills, experience, and demand. Also consider, this number assumes you're working every billable hour you have available. That might not be the case if you have slow months.

How to Flat Rate Quote

Here's the equation:

    Estimated Hours to Execute at Your Hourly Rate

+   Estimated Management Hours at Your Hourly Rate

+/- Size of the Client

+/- Value of the Project to the Client

+/- Extent of Use (Licensing)

+/- Demand for Your Work

+/- Timeline

+/- Buffer (because shit happens)

=   Your flat rate

Let's go into that a little deeper:

How many hours do you expect you'll spend on creative work for the project? Remember that flat rates require a defined scope. Consider time for initial work as well as whatever revision/edit rounds you're including. Multiply that number by your hourly rate. This is a good starting point for your flat rate. Now for the important part. Adjust this number based on the following factors.

How many hours will you need for project management? Depending on the project, management can take up to 50% of the total time! Plan for these hours. This includes meetings, phone calls, conference calls (Yuck. Gag), making contracts, sending invoices, sending status updates, preparing proofs, reviewing changes, clarifying client feedback, etc..

How big is the client that you are quoting, and what is the value of the project to the client? Are they a global corporation with a huge market and audience, or a mom and pop shop with only a regional clientele? Their reach will impact your price. Keep in mind: not every client is a good fit for you. They might be too small to afford your rates. Try and learn about the client, their revenue streams, the goals of the project, and the target demographic. This will shed light on how valuable the project is to a client. An internal flier for Coca-Cola's employee softball team is much different than an external flier for a holiday sale. The softball flier reaches a very limited demographic, and doesn't result in any revenue for the company. The holiday sale flier reaches the vast audience of Coca-Cola buyers, and results in huge revenue. Your flat rate for each flier will be very different because of these factors, even though it will take the same time and materials to do both.

To what extent will your work be used by the client? Just online, just for a seasonal campaign, on all 25 franchise location windows? The more use it gets, the more value it has to the client and the more it should cost.

Is it a full buyout of your work (meaning they own the work in full and can use it to any extent, perpetually, exclusively), or is the client just licensing the work from you for limited use? Logos and identity work are great examples of full buyout projects. These are instances where the client should be the sole owner of the work, and be able to use it exclusively in perpetuity. However, there's a way to sell certain kinds of creative work to multiple people without losing your ownership of the work. Which means there's opportunity to make profit off the work over and over again for the foreseeable future. It's called licensing. Licensing is when you allow a client the right to use your work for a limited amount of time and/or a limited extent (sometimes for a specific quantity of units, on a very specific product, and in a specific region). You remain the owner of the work's copyright, only allowing limited use to the client for a flat fee, royalties, or a mix of both. When you see a *Star Wars* character on a Stance sock, the image of that character is just being licensed to Stance for that limited product. Lucasfilm Ltd. remains the owner of the copyright. Lucasfilm Ltd. didn't sell the work's ownership to Stance, otherwise Lucasfilm Ltd. wouldn't be able to also license those characters to other companies to make other products with them. You could license a photo for limited use on a book cover, license an illustration for limited use on a tote bag, license your book for a film adaptation.

If you're licensing your work to someone, be sure to clarify the extent. Do yourself a favor and look up Jessica Hische's article about licensing and pricing on her site. Also, the Graphic Artists Guild has a great article called "License It" on their website that sheds some serious light on the issue. Your business lawyer will be a great resource on this topic, as well.

Is your work in high demand? Then you can justifiably raise your rates. Your time and talents are a limited commodity.

Do you have time, and does the client want the project done fast? If you already have a booked schedule and someone asks you for a quote, this can be an opportunity to ask for more. You don't need the job. Maybe you don't even want it. So make the flat rate quote a number that would justify the late nights and stress. Use it as an opportunity to test higher pricing. Likewise, if a client wants a job done quicker than usual, then charge a rush fee. Same if someone wants work done over a weekend.

Refer to industry guides. For designers: The *Graphic Artists Guild's Handbook: Pricing & Ethical Guidelines* is a great reference for pricing. You might not make those rates immediately, but it is a great goal to work towards. Aim for a rate that is both fair for your client, and fair to you (representative of your skill, experience level, and needs).

Your turn! Flat Rate Quote Three Services

Choose three services you do regularly (or plan to do), and scope them. Meaning, write down the clear parameters of what the rate includes. How many initial proof options will the client get, how many revision rounds, what final deliverables? Then use the Flat Rate Formula from the previous pages to come up with a baseline price. Calculate it for the average client you expect to get.

Service #1

Service #2

Service #3

To Free or Not to Free

Some creatives are adamantly against doing free work. However, we think that in very rare circumstances (emphasis on very), it can be okay and even exciting. Just be cautious on how you give these freebies away and who you give them to. It should be someone that you hope to build credit with, or someone/something you know well and want to invest in.

The Case for Doing Free Work:

- You get to stipulate that the work done is your gift, therefore subject to your style and whims (client feedback not allowed or very minimal). You get to play Creative Director and are in complete control of the end product. Of course, you shouldn't use the freedom against the client's best interests. The freedom should still be subject to making something that works for the brand you are creating for.

- You get to potentially help a friend, charity, or family member out with a job. This either makes you feel good or racks up valuable IOUs for the future.

- You get to work on a project you're passionate about.

- If you do offer someone free work, stipulate in the deal that they promote you in return. For example: You create a logo for them, and in return they give you a designer credit in the footnote of their website with a link to your portfolio site, they promote you 3 times on their various social media platforms, and once in their weekly newsletter. This could result in new business leads for you from their audience. It's a great way to make a one sided deal into a win win for everyone.

The Case Against Free Work:

- If you don't get something out of the free work, you will most likely find yourself feeling resentful and used. This could impact relationships.

- You risk miss-educating the person on the value of the work you are doing. Be sure if you do free work for someone, that you first explain the value of it, what you would normally charge someone, and what a heck of a deal you are giving them. The key here is making them feel the value of your service. Hopefully, one day, they will be able to pay it back in some form, knowing what you invested.

- You don't want someone telling everyone they know that you're the dummy who works for free. The person you donate work to should know how you prefer them to talk about your working arrangement. Either have them phrase it as being a charitable donation, or be sure they know the real price you charge so they can tell any inquiring minds.

Unless it's a straight up gift or donation, almost everyone has something they can barter for your services. Don't let yourself be used and abused out of pity, especially if someone has something you'd be willing to trade for. If you can, get the other person to have some skin in the game. Find something you can trade them for so they have a proportionate understanding of the value of the work.

Perceived Value vs. Cost

The goal of smart pricing, is to price based on the value of your work, not just on the exact cost of the services rendered. The value of your work is somewhat subjective. You have to find a balance between what you think a project is worth, and what the project is worth to the client. Your goal is to present yourself as a valuable asset with invaluable skills and experience. How do you know what those worthy attributes are? Listen to your potential and existing clients. When new people connect with you, why do they reach out? Because of a referral who loves your attitude and reliability? Because they saw your work and think you are the only one who can achieve the look they want? What are those things worth to them?

Winning projects on cheap prices alone is risky and leaves you with a mercurial clientele who will drop you the minute they find a better deal. Rather, focus on educating your clients on your value, something that validates paying more for you and remaining loyal to you. Usually that value lies in reliability, trustworthiness, your ability to deliver high-quality work, or a knack for understanding their company's unique brand style and voice. If you can be attentive and deliver things that matter to your clients, you will have no problem slowly building your rates to the level you want and deserve.

Be careful not to define the worth of your services in the vacuum of your own opinion. Your opinion is just as important as your audience's. If the majority of your potential clients are turning your quotes down, your price does not match their perceived value of what you do, rightly or wrongly. So you have two choices: either lower your price, or work on educating your clients (prospective and existing) on the value of what you do. Maybe the only reason they won't pay your prices is because you haven't made the case for it through your own brand messaging. Be on the ball. Take hold of the opportunities to explain why you do what you do, and what goes into it. When someone requests a quote, set up a call to talk them through it, instead of simply delivering it in an email, so you can answer any big misconceptions or miscommunications right away.

Find ways to better explain the value and quality you can offer. Use your website as a platform to educate clients on your worth and expertise before they even hire you. Let your previous clients speak for you through testimonials. Let your work speak for you through case studies that really reveal the success of a project and the depth of the process. Portfolio photos are great, but the real value is the creative thinking behind it all—the who, what, why, and how.

How did the project make your client more money? How did it raise awareness? How did it lead to a spike in subscribers? These are the things that show that your creative work is not just something pretty, but something that solved a problem.

Raising your Rates

At the beginning of your creative career (or maybe even at the beginning of your freelance career), your rate will likely be lower than you want it to be. You are just trying to win new clients, build a portfolio, and gain experience. This is often referred to as "paying your dues," but don't worry, it doesn't have to last forever! In fact, it should be as brief as possible. Constantly test the boundaries of your rates, growing it in step with your experience, client roster, and talent. Don't stay in the same pricing model because you're scared. Raise your rates regularly (in justifiable increments). Worst case scenario, you negotiate the price and scope down to keep a client who was not willing to pay the new rate (if you really need the money or are really interested in the project/client) or you count your losses and let the client walk (if you don't need the money and feel it's the right time for both parties to part ways). Best case scenario, they say, "yes!" and you learn that the client's perception of your value is in match with yours. Never let fear guide your pricing. Base pricing on fair calculations of time, materials, demand, and value.

Signs That You Should Raise Your Prices:

a. **The inquiring client is a larger name or company than you usually work with.** If you've been pricing based on the budgets of local businesses and family friends, when a Fortune 500 company comes calling, don't give them the same rate you've been using. Understand that you need to adjust for the larger influence and audience of the larger brand. The work is worth much more to a brand that services billions of people, than a company that has an audience of only thousands. Plus, a lot more time and work can go into getting all the necessary approvals when working with a company of that size.

b. **They want you to "do you".** If you start getting quote requests because of a unique style that you are becoming known for, then this is added value. It's the difference between paying for a DaVinci knockoff and a genuine masterpiece. If your style is rare and not easily imitable, that makes your value even higher.

c. **You're getting more work than you can handle.** If so many people are saying "yes" to your quotes that you have to live off of 3 hours of sleep and work nights and weekends, then raise your prices. You are underestimating your worth and demand. Adjust for your limited resources (time, creativity and sanity) and the growing demand for your work.

When you raise your prices, you will likely lose some clients, but you can refer them to trusted creative peers who are looking for work to ensure your former client is still in good hands once they leave you. The clients that remain on your roster will be willing to pay your higher rates because they understand your value and demand. By moving some clients on, you're making room for new clients with bigger budgets. Way to go, friend, that's growing your business! This is how you gradually move from working a lot for a little, to working a little for a lot. This is not taking advantage, but leveraging your skills for the best return. With bigger clients on the books, you might choose to take a few passion projects on for less, but only as they appeal to your interests and convictions.

Feast & Famine

Your pricing might have to fluctuate based on things out of your control. Depending on the state of the economy, or perhaps just an unpredictably slow month, you might take on work at a lower rate than usual to keep money coming in. If it's a slow season and people are declining your normal rates, but you want money coming in, counter-offer a reduced rate for a revised project scope. This is a compromise that might win you back the job without cheapening your value or services. This is nothing to be ashamed of. This is adapting to changing economies.

The alternative? You can stick to the value of your services regardless. If you have a nest egg built up, this might be fine as you ride out slower months. But be on guard. If you go through consistent months where no one is accepting your proposals, reconsider your pricing or how you're communicating value. Sticking to your guns might stick you out of business if you're not careful.

Quote Request Responses

Just because someone emails or calls asking you for a quote, doesn't mean you have to send them one. For every interested party, you have a range of optional responses:

a. **"Thanks for your interest! I'd love to talk more about your project on the phone so I can more accurately quote this…"** This response is for serious inquiries that you want to take the time to vet before quoting. These are the ones you want to ask about their company, project scope, project outcome goals, and budget.

b. **"We're honored you considered us for your creative needs! However, we're not currently taking on new clients."** Perhaps their values or product don't align with yours. Perhaps you see red flags that hint they will be an unreasonable client. Perhaps you're just plain not interested in what they're doing.

c. **"Thanks for thinking of me on your project. Based on your description, I think I might know someone more fitted for your needs…"** If you don't think the person can afford you, if you don't offer the requested service, or you don't think their project or style aligns with you, but you know a fellow creative who does fit, try and give a referral. We have all kinds of freelance friends at different levels and with different aesthetics. Each one has a nice niche. It can be hard to find work, and on the client end, it can be hard to find good creatives. If you can connect the right people it will come back in spades, even if not right away. Plus, that creative peer will most likely do the same for you when the opportunity arises.

d. **"Thanks for telling me about your project. Based on your information, I prepared a proposal for you, which is attached. Look it over and let's talk more about it sometime this week!"** If the person inquiring has already given you enough info to quote on and it seems like a business-as-usual type of project, then just go ahead and send the proposal. For some situations, you really want to wow them, and sending an email with an attached deck just isn't enough. If you can't get to them in person, arrange a phone call where you can set the tone before you go over the price quote and proposal with them. You're not just giving them a price, you're presenting yourself as someone who can solve their unique problem.

e. **"Can you send me more details on what your project is, what company it is for, and what your budget is? My schedule is fairly busy, so I'll need to know these things before I can call you to talk more."** If someone emails you something like "Hi, I need a website. How much is it? Call me ASAP," then you are justified in grilling them for the needed information to even consider whether you want to quote them. This kind of email usually reveals a few things about this potential client: they don't understand design/photography/copyediting/etc.. enough to know that they need to send you much more information to get a quote on this kind of project, they aren't used to working with creatives, they value their time more than yours (being as they took no time to give you context, and yet want you to jump to accommodate their needs), they probably haven't thought much about their project, and they underestimate how much time and money will be involved. With potential clients, it's key to establish early on that you expect well-thought-out emails and respect for your time. You can communicate this by responding similar to our example above. If the person doesn't respond well to this prompting, and can't take time to send you the basic outline of their request, they're not going to become any easier to work with down the road. Save yourself the headache and avoid clients who don't show respect or professionalism.

Project Proposals: More than a Quote

While a quote is just a dollar amount with a scope, a proposal is the way you contextualize your quote to show the value behind it. This is where you prove why you're the right fit for the client, and how you can help solve their unique problem.

In our experience, a good proposal for a project includes a simple and clear outline of the project goal, notes on how you want to approach the project to best meet their needs and appeal to their audience (a teaser, don't give away the farm), an outline of proposed scope, an estimated timeline (if possible), some work examples of similar projects, a quote (ballpark or exact, depending on how much info you have from them), and any important terms.

These proposals can be time consuming, even if you're using a template, so only make them once you've vetted the prospective client and project on the phone or by email. Do research on people inquiring for your services and see if you can find out more about them. Try and weed out non-serious inquiries from promising potentials. You can learn a lot about someone and their project by a quick phone call and the right questions.

Questions to Ask Potential Clients to Prepare a Fair Quote and Tailored Proposal:

1. What are your company's goals within the next few years?

2. What would be the best result of this project, in your opinion? What is the purpose you hope it will achieve? What would failure look like?

3. Who is the target audience for this project?

4. If the project is re-doing something that exists, why is the old solution no longer working? Knowing what doesn't work will inform what changes need to be made.

5. Who at your company will be involved with this project? It's good to know how many cooks will be in the kitchen. Who has final approval? How many levels of sign-offs need to be obtained to launch, etc.?

6. What is your budget for this project?

7. What are your company's main products/services right now, and how will this project relate to them? How do you expect this project to affect or generate growth/sales, if at all?

8. Do you have a deadline or time frame you're trying to complete this project within? If they give you a really tight window, then you can consider working a rush fee into the price.

You get the idea. These kinds of questions will help you better identify how serious your client is, to what scale they're doing business, and how realistic their hopes are for the outcome of your work. Now you know how to tailor your proposal to their outlook.

The money questions might feel awkward to ask, but they are very important. While the potential client genuinely might not know what they're willing to budget, you need to try and probe them for honest financial cues to help you gauge a fair price for them. If they are annoyed or wary when you ask these things, then take note. This might reveal a distrustful nature. Generally, seasoned or serious professionals should be comfortable talking honestly about budgets to a reasonable extent. Most companies should know what kind of money they have budgeted for marketing, design, etc.. Most mid-size to large companies have to share this sort of information with their shareholders, anyway. Usually, smaller companies are the ones who get a little antsy about sharing this data. In these situations, you can usually tell what kind of budget they have by the size of their business and the type of product or service they offer. Asking questions about the kind of work and clients they have can tell you a lot about their financial range without sounding nosy. Find a tactful and honest way to approach it. This is key information for offering a proposal that's right for them.

Sometimes a meeting is key to properly present your proposal. Other times an email is plenty. If the project is small and for someone you've already worked with, you might skip the proposal stage and just present your pricing in a simple email.

How to Make Your Quote Resonate Both Conversationally and Within a Designed Proposal:

1. Show that you understand the client's business model, goals, and values. If they're going to trust their project with you, someone they likely don't know very well, then you have to show that you deserve their trust. Invest time in understanding who they are before they've even paid you. Customize the presentation to speak in terms of their unique goals and brand voice. Quoting isn't just about the right price. It's about understanding their culture and business.

2. Show how you can meet their expectations for the project. Every potential client has an idea in their head of what a good outcome would look like. At the very least, they know what a terrible outcome is. Ask them about what they want to achieve through the work you're quoting for. Do they want to increase their sales by x% through a new campaign that promotes their whole product line? Do they want to raise awareness in an under-served demographic of their industry? Do they want to create something that will appeal to potential investors? Knowing the client's terms for success will help you communicate value better in your quote presentation.

3. Translate the price into the client's own industry currency. When you talk about the quote amount, try and relate that cost to the client's own revenue stream, if it helps justify the cost. For example, we once quoted a photographer on a logo design. When we sent the proposal and quote, the photographer scoffed at the amount, saying it was, "way out of their budget." So the next time a photographer asked for a logo request, we added context to the cost in terms the photographer could relate to. We wrote something to the effect of: "The cost of this logo design package is an investment in your brand presence, setting a tone for your visual messaging for the lifespan of your business. While the value of a good logo is priceless, we've quoted it in a way that we know will be supportable by your business. You'll likely be able to pay off this investment by booking one or two wedding shoots." Another good example is when we quoted a brewery restaurant on a new brand identity package that included a logo, messaging, website, packaging and more. While the cost might seem high outside of context, we explained that it could be paid off by one good month of business if they only got X amount of customers in the door drinking one beer each. We admitted that we understood we were not their only expense. But showing how quickly the cost could be recuperated in these simple terms helped them grasp the large sum in perspective to its reward.

4. Show proof of your successes in similar projects previously. Prove that this isn't your first rodeo. Give evidence that you have conquered a similar task successfully before. Shed light on your process and organization to show that you know how to manage many moving parts all at once. Reference any recognizable brands or companies you have worked with, reminding the potential client you belong at the table.

5. Set the scene, gain trust, then deliver the quote (the proposal anatomy). Don't put the quote at the beginning of your proposal. Build up to it. Set the mood right and your price will look justified, not startling. Begin with a nice cover page customized to them. Include their name, the project the quote is for, and the date of delivery. Next, concisely explain the main purpose of the project, and any associated goals. This should mirror all the points the client explained to you on the phone. This shows that you heard them and understand their needs. While there might be one main problem to address, there are often a handful of goals that must coincide to result in your desired solution. Goals often reflect the simultaneous needs of a company's owners, workers, audience, and investors. Next, prove that you are the right person for the job. Show what skills and methods you want to employ. Explain your inspiration at a high level (don't give away the farm). Show examples of similar work you have done before. Lastly, outline the scope (be as specific as possible) and price quote.

Add an expiration date. Protect yourself and add a sense of urgency by putting an expiration date on the proposal. It can be in fine print on the bottom of each page, or at the bottom of the cover sheet. Ours simply says "This quote expires within 30 days of delivery." This will let the potential client know that they can't sit on this forever and then return to you in 2 years and say they want to move forward. It motivates them to make a decision a little faster, while also giving you the option to charge more if they come back after your rates have changed. What sounds like a reasonable price to you now could look a lot different in a year when your client roster is stacked.

Proposal Templates

Always look for ways to make your non-creative tasks more efficient. Early on we realized that building quote proposals is a big time suck. Is it important? Yes. Very. But was it taking too much time out of our design day? Yes. So we created template proposals that beautifully presented our most commonly requested services. The proposal answers all the potential client's biggest questions, which creates a sense of trust from the start.

Our deck (fancy word for presentation) starts with a proposal cover page customized to the client, then goes into an overview of our process, presents relevant portfolio work examples, explains the deliverables, general timetable, scope, and finally, the price quote. Each page has our logo and contact info in the footer so someone can easily follow up.

Now, when someone writes in to request a quote for branding, we just go into the template for that service, customize the few points that change per client, export the PDF, and send. This saves so much time compared to writing out a unique explanation of the same information each time. This presentation deck shouldn't replace interacting with the client entirely, but it does save time by covering the basics and prepping the client to understand the process and value in what you do. People sometimes write back to just tell us how impressed they are with our pricing presentation. This is one of those ways to prove your worth and level of professionalism. It's an education point that can set the right expectations. If you don't have the time or bandwidth to make your own, you can buy our Proposal Template here: www.hoodzpahdesign.com/product/project-proposal-template.

Chapter Checklist: To Do

- ☐ Calculate your hourly rate using the worksheet on page 51.
- ☐ Scope out and flat rate price your 3 most common services on page 54.
- ☐ Create a quote proposal template.

*Another blank page in case
you want to tear out the poster
on the next page.*

But also...

is the emptiness

making anyone else

feel existential?

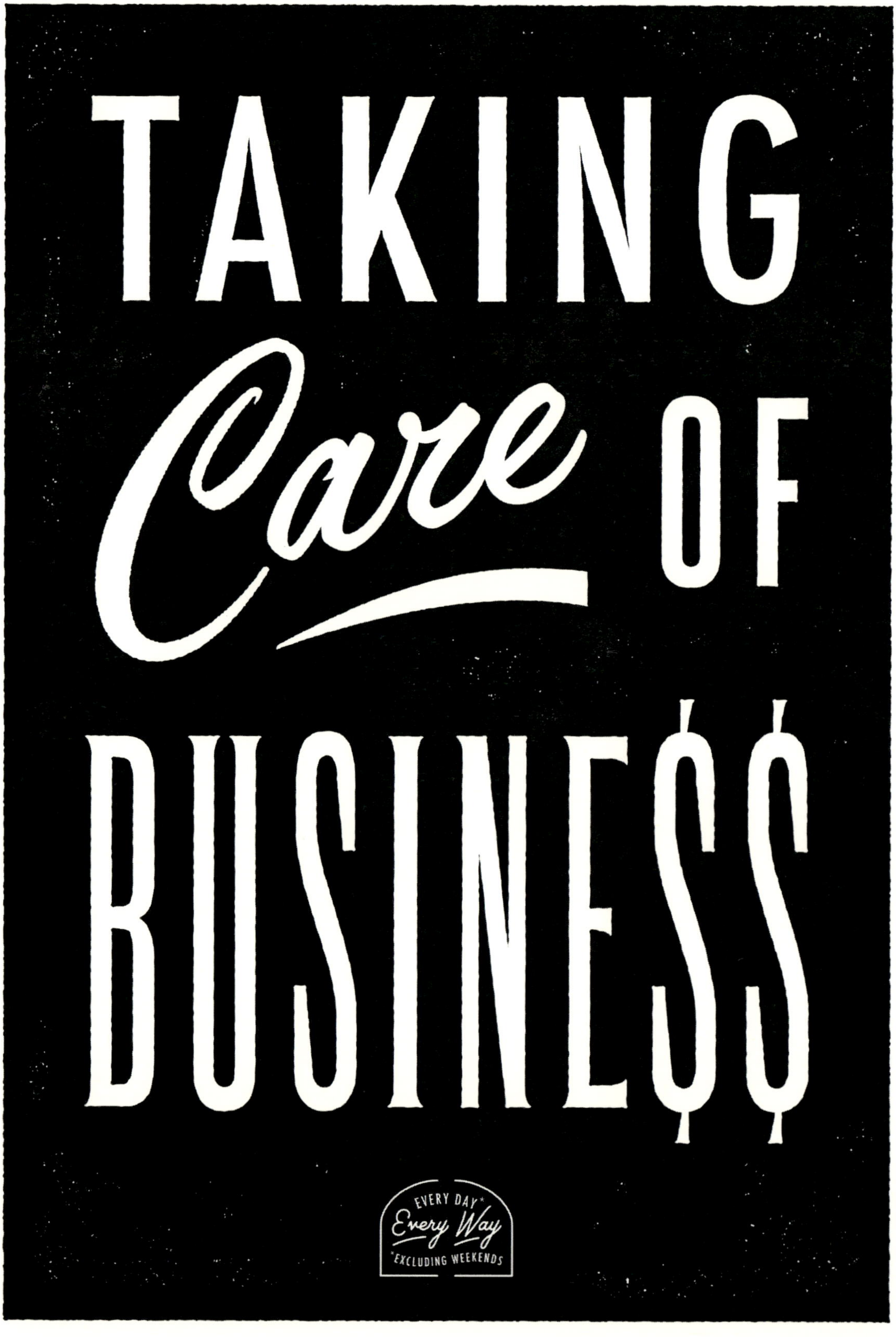

Illustration by Amy Hood of Hoodzpah (Hoodzpahdesign.com)

5

How to Create a Business Plan

How playing The Oregon Trail *and losing little Susie to dysentery applies to business forecasting.*

———

You want to start your own creative business. You're still reading this book after four chapters. We admire your persistence. However, to make sure you're not operating solely on blind confidence, let's create a business plan. Don't get us wrong, naive ego can go a long way (thanks to all the parents out there who told us we could do anything and be anything), but faith without work is death. You need a realistic plan and a roadmap to get to your goal. Anyone can start their own business. Achieving profitability and consistently growing to meet new goals is another matter entirely.

A business plan adds flesh and bones to your as-yet-vague-dream of independence. It's the equivalent of mapping your route along the Oregon Trail before you ever get in the wagon. There are inquiries and calculations to be made before you start. You need to be sure you know how much food you'll need, where you'll stop to rest, who will drive when, how long it will take, how much ground you need to cover per day to get to your destination before winter sets in, what first aid provisions to bring so Susie doesn't die of dysentery, when you'll caulk the wagon and float it, how you'll make ends meet along the way, and how much the whole thing will cost up front. It's an exercise in trying to look at the end from the beginning. There needs to be a clear and obtainable goal to motivate you through the treacherous passes and torrential waters.

A business plan is not a crystal ball. And as sad as we are about it, you're not Miss Cleo. Or are you? Miss Cleo, if you're reading this book, please email us a testimonial to include on the dust jacket of the hard copy. Everybody else, you're normal people who cannot know the future. That's okay. A business plan is not meant to be an unalterable, exact picture of your future business. It's more of a possible road map, and that's a good enough starting point to prove potential. You'll update and revise your business plan as you go along. Just like your budget, it's meant to be revisited and revised as you learn and grow. Things will change and morph as you know and experience more. This is why it's referred to as a "living document." A business plan typically makes projections across three to five years. When we started Hoodzpah, we started small. We made a one-year plan. It was all we could wrap our heads around with so many uncertainties, but even that was enough to give us a good idea of how and where to start.

If there's one tip we could give before you dive in to this: just start. You can change things later and this isn't written in stone or tattooed forever. Just rely on what you know for sure now and ask friends or peers for help on the few unknowns you have left. There is no one right answer. As with creativity, there are many right answers. Again, we say, just start! So much will become clearer once you've gotten your feet wet and actually start to do business. Planning is potential. Doing is realization.

*

HOODZPAH HOT-TAKE

Just start... Things will change and morph as you know and experience more.

Now check your dread at the door, because we're going to walk through the basics of creating a business plan together. This is not a rigid structure. Tailor it to your needs. If something doesn't apply to you, skip it. If you get stuck on a point, just move on and come back to it later when you've got a few other things figured out. If a question keeps hanging you up, reach out to a business mentor or a trusty friend. Sometimes the very act of explaining a problem out loud is enough to help you find an answer. Open up a blank word doc or notebook page and write bullet points as you read through the following sections. What you jot down will be what we use to write your final business plan. Let's get started!

Company Overview

1. What is the business name and legal status?

Sole Proprietor, Partnership, Corporation, or Limited Liability Corporation (LLC)? Refer to *Chapter 7 - Making it Official* if you're unsure which business structure is best for you. If you haven't named your company yet, go to the section titled "Name and Tagline" in *Chapter 6 - Branding Your Business*.

2. Who are you?

Introduce yourself and any partners you have in your new creative business. What is your professional history? What are your individual qualifications? What is your education and experience in this field? You might think it's awkward to talk about yourself on paper, but get used to pumping your own ego tires, it's a big part of running your own business. Trust: talking about your achievements and positive qualities doesn't make you a blow-hard as long as you keep the tone friendly and the length succinct. Keep it to key highlights that reveal your professional strengths and winning personality. This is an exercise you'll have to repeat again and again as a business owner. You need to be able to introduce yourself and relay your selling points confidently and quickly.

3. What kind of professional support system do you have?

Do you have advisors and outside help? If so, what are their roles and to what extent? What are their qualifications? A credible advisor can lend experience to a new outfit that will give comfort to investors and bankers. Refer back to the A-team we assembled in Chapter 2. If you are making a physical product, who is your manufacturing outfit? If you're making a digital product, who is your development team? If you will require a staff, what type of individuals will you hire and what qualifications will they have? And so on.

Business Offering

1. What will your services menu be?

List the services you'll provide and their prices. Describe their scope and estimate their price (either flat rate or a window of time charged at an hourly rate). What makes your services unique and competitive in comparison to those of the established competition?

2. What products, if any, will you offer?

List the products, their price, and your method of selling (in store and/or online, direct to consumer and/or wholesale).

Market Research

1. Who are your clients?

Describe both your current clients and your dream clients. If you can find financial statistics about your audience, their disposable income and spending priorities, definitely include that. Your goal is to prove that there are people who need what you offer, and have the income to support your prices. For your dream clients, explain their culture and values, and how you and your services fit into that. If there is a unique demographic you plan to appeal to, explain that.

2. What is the market demand for your services?

Can you prove that there is a need for your skills and services? Then show that. If businesses similar to yours have succeeded, profile those instances. Include any research you can find proving companies / people are in need of your unique services. If there is a new or underserved industry that you aim to serve, explain that.

3. Competitive Landscape?

What is the competitive landscape like in your industry/field? Companies that prove your business model—will they also draw from the same client pool as you? Show your competitive edge on those companies. Find information on their pricing, service offering, personality, and method of doing business so you can carve out a niche for yourself apart from them. What are their strengths, weaknesses, opportunities, and threats (SWOT)? What are yours by comparison? Start marking your territory.

Marketing Strategy

1. How are you going to reach potential customers?

Advertising? Sending promotional materials or capabilities books with work samples out in the mail? Cold emails? Social media? Your own website? Include a list of the ways you plan to get the word out. Here are some marketing avenues to consider when drafting this section:

- a. Social Media
- b. Networking Events and Trade Shows
- c. Online and Print Advertising
- d. Referral Program - Reward those who send you work
- e. Incentive Program - Encourage repeat clients
- f. Cross Promoting with Products and Brands that Complement (but don't conflict)

2. What resources will you need to execute your marketing strategy?

Keep in mind that you don't have to have a huge cash budget for marketing initially. There's so much that can be done to promote yourself on social media or in person for $$Free$$! You just have to be willing to put in the time. Organic growth of your audience can be slow going at first, but with unique and genuine attention to the platforms and opportunities at hand, it can begin to gather its own forward momentum.

*

HOODZPAH HOT-TAKE

Beware income monogamy. Diversify your revenue streams.

Financial Plan

Define your revenue goals and estimated expenses by answering the below questions. Luckily, we answered almost all of these questions in *Chapter 3 - Making A Budget* and *Chapter 4 - Pricing & Proposals*. Refer back to those if you need.

a. What is your planned take-home income or salary?

   b. What are your estimated business expenses?

   c. Based on that, what does your company need to make in revenue its first year?

   d. What will you charge (flat rate and hourly)?

   e. How much will you need to work or how many products/services will you need to sell to meet your revenue goal? Try to estimate how much money you'll make from your various revenue streams. How much of that work do you estimate will be from existing clients versus new clients?

At Hoodzpah, our core service is brand identity, so we work with a lot of new clients. But many of our clients end up becoming repeat clients for ongoing projects and needs. We plan for about a 50/50 split in new versus returning clients. As far as product/service planning, we estimate for 30% of our yearly revenue to be new brand identity packages. Another 35% is made up of secondary services (illustration, production work, packaging work). Speaking and workshops accounts for 10%. Lastly, 25-ish% of our revenue is made from product sales. We sell things like fonts, mock-ups (and other design downloads), this book you're reading, and other odds and sods. These estimations are based on trends and data we track in our accounting software. That's our monthly revenue breakdown, or at least what we aim for. Things fluctuate per month, of course.

The main thing is to beware revenue monogamy. You don't want to rely solely on one cash cow client for 80% of your work. Why? If you lose them, you could be at risk of losing your whole business. Keep a happy balance of new and repeat customers. If you can, set up retainer agreements with the steady clients you do ongoing work for. You should also begin to think of ways you can make more passive income through products. As creatives, our revenue is mainly based on services rendered, meaning we only make money for the time we're working. If you can make a product once, and then sell it many times with minimal effort ongoing, you are beginning to find ways to make money without having to work for every hour. A great example is a digital product to sell that can be directly downloaded by your user. You spent the time to create something once that many customers can download (unlike hard goods) and you can just watch the dollars stack up in your bank account. Of course, it's not exactly that easy. There is occasional maintenance and customer service, but it can be a much less time-consuming form of revenue if you find the right product to make and the right demand exists.

Executive Summary

Once you've filled in answers for all the previous sections and questions that apply to you, go back through and weave the bullet points you've written into short paragraphs. Remember that you're not trying to win at Scrabble and you're not getting paid by the word. The key is to get your plan across simply and clearly. On the first pass, don't try to be smart or witty or even professional, just make complete sentences, keeping things organized and in their respective sections. After you've done that, then you can go back through the draft again to weave in your personality and voice. Re-read and refine until you find it satisfactory, sending off to a friend for critique. Congratulations, you've got a neatly organized roadmap with clear goals and set benchmarks for yourself! Your business plan is almost done! Now, for the final piece: The Executive Summary.

This section is the first one that will appear in your final business plan, but we are writing it last having done all the busy work first. The Executive Summary is the trailer to the feature film. You've jotted down a lot of information above, probably pages and pages. The executive summary takes all of that info and gives a one page short synopsis in its place. If someone doesn't have time to read your whole plan, they should be able to get the gist of things from the Executive Summary at the beginning. Traditionally, this section is no more than two pages, but if you can get the point across in less, more power to you. Wax long or wax short, just wax.

What is your Value Proposition Statement?

This is the 30 second answer you give to that awful question, "What do you do?" You can arrive at this by distilling your Executive Summary even further to its most condensed and powerful sentence (or two). It should include what your product/service is, why it's valuable to your consumer, and why they should pick you over the competition.

Chapter Checklist: To Do

Now you're ready to gather all the information you've written down and layout your finalized business plan so you can show it to potential investors, banks you're trying to convince to give you a loan, and your Mom. Here's how we'd organize it:

- ☐ Executive Summary
- ☐ Company Overview: Name and Business Structure, Value Proposition Statement, Who Are You?, Professional Support System
- ☐ Business Offering: Services, Products
- ☐ Market Research: Your Consumer Base, Market Demand, Competitive Landscape
- ☐ Marketing Strategy: Reaching Your Potential Consumer, Resources to Accomplish That
- ☐ Financial Plan

Yet another blank page in case you want to tear out the poster on the next page.

But also,

an abstract painting of

a Boston winter;

The white's of your dream client's eyes as they behold the splendor of your first proof;

The glint of Dwayne "the Rock" Johnson's luminous teeth;

The glow of that initial payment check;

The hopeful expanse of a blank Illustrator file - full of promise and potential;

The sheen of your keyboard upon cleaning it for the first time (after 3 years of ownership).

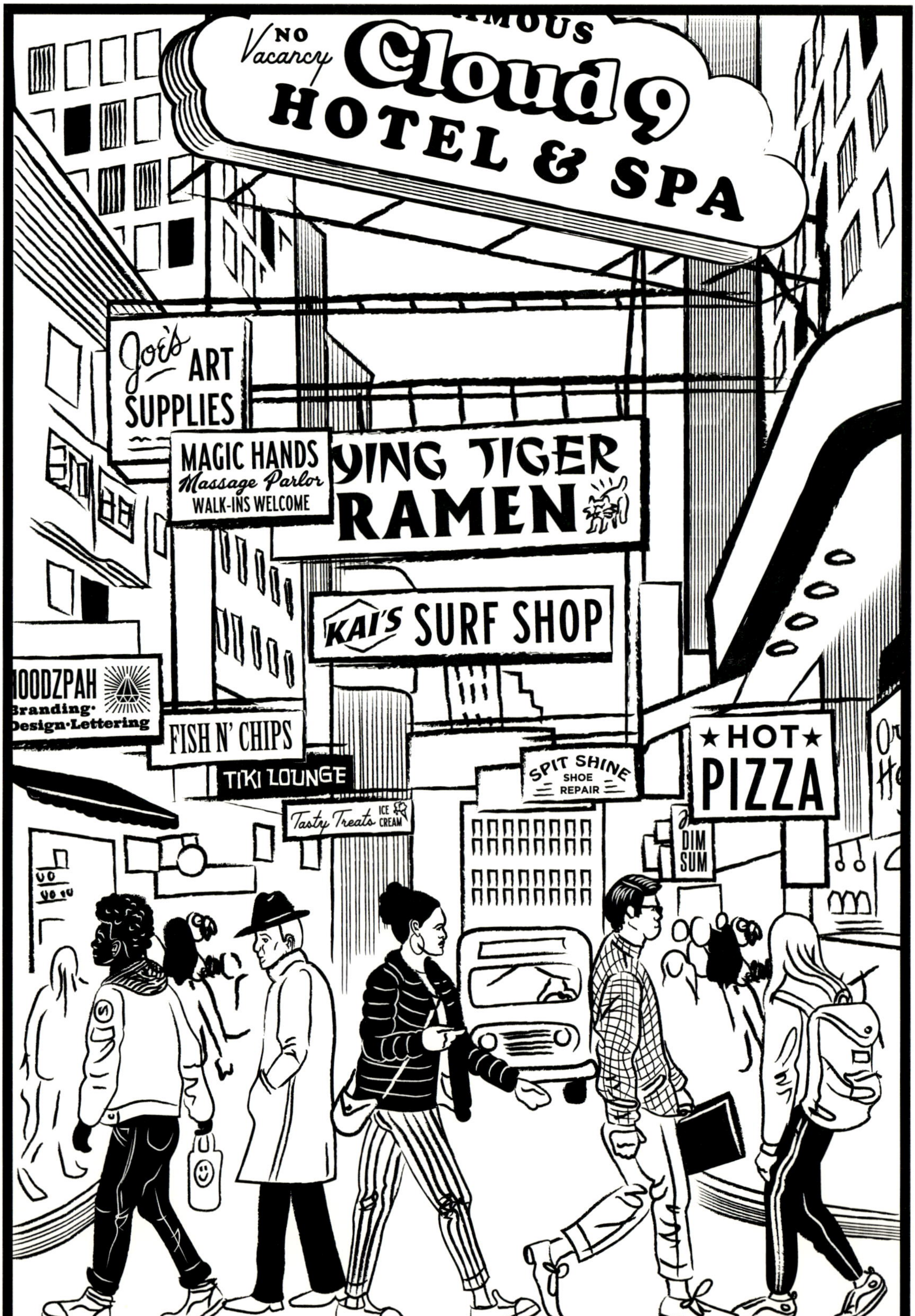

Illustration by Amy Hood of Hoodzpah (Hoodzpahdesign.com)

6
Branding Your Business

*People may choose a book by its cover,
but they keep reading for the plot.*

———

The word "branding" has become as confusing and misused as the word "literally". No, you don't literally want to eat a cute baby (or at least we hope not), and no, you didn't literally almost die when you went through a whole day with a dandruff flake in your eyebrow. Curb your superlatives! "Branding" is one of those words creatives throw around just as casually. Some use "branding" synonymously with "identity" and "logo". We've been just as guilty of this. So while we preach to ourselves, we'll also preach to you.

What is a Brand, Identity, and Logo?

Here's a quick crash course before we dive in deeper.

A brand is a relationship between your company and the world. It's how people perceive your company based on their experience with you (indirectly or directly). A brand isn't your logo or your business cards or your website. Rather, these are piece's of your brand's identity. As an example, Wells Fargo has the same logo and identity system today as it did in 2015. But today, unlike then, we know that the company opened millions of unauthorized accounts for customers and forced insurance on people who didn't need it. The perception of their brand has completely shifted from positive to negative. So now, their logo carries negative connotations (despite being exactly the same logo). In an opposite example: Kia entered the American market as a "cheap" car. The product didn't deliver a great experience to users. But over the past decade, the company has strategically turned the narrative around by focusing on quality. By bettering the user's experience, the brand has gone from being the "bummer" car, into the hit blue-collar car that beats luxury competitors in industry rankings.

A brand identity is similar to how it sounds. Something's identity is defined by signature characteristics that make it uniquely *it*. A brand identity is the collection of characteristics that help the world recognize it: fonts, colors, tone of voice, aesthetic style. Just like a person, your brand has unique features and mannerisms that unfold across your website, social media, tone of messaging, logo mark and so on. The goal is to keep these features consistent so the world continues to recognize you every time they experience your brand. If you're constantly putting on disguises and playing other parts, no one will remember you and what you stand for.

A logo is a graphic and/or typographic mark that identifies your company. Your logo is one part of your brand identity. It is meaningless without consistent context and experience. But it is powerful beyond measure when it becomes synonymous with the positive feelings people have about a brand.

Logos are funny things. At first they are just designs on paper. Eventually they come to embody all the qualities of the organization they represent, and most people cannot separate the "design" from their full range of opinions about the organization. The hard task the designer faces is trying to help the client see how the logo might eventually be perceived, how it will work for them, not just whether they "like it".

- Tom Geismar, graphic designer and a founding partner of Chermayeff & Geismar & Haviv, in an interview with LogoDesignLove.com

The 90% You Can't See: Brand

Like the universe, a brand is 90% dark matter. It's there and it's important, but it's intangible. Your brand is a combination of the story you tell and your audience's reaction to that story. It's a collaboration between you and the world experiencing you. A brand isn't something you can completely control. When you start your business, you will attempt to target a certain audience through a specific aesthetic and tone. It will be purely your vision. And then the collaboration begins. As a user experiences your company, they will assign to it emotions based on personal experiences or passive impressions; and you will adapt accordingly, either by trying to shift the perception or by using the perception more to your advantage. It's a give and take, a jam session that never ends. At its best, the audience response helps reveal your brand and company's greatest strengths. In harder times, it reveals cracks in your systems and services. The good part is that a brand evolves. It has a life with life stages, the occasional mid-life crisis, and even moments of apotheosis.

The experience people have with your business/service/product is key. The brand identity and story need to prepare people for this experience, set their expectations, and excite them about what's to come. Then it's up to your company to deliver on that expectation. To do business well, you can't have one without the other. A beautiful brand identity with a poor product or bad service won't create a loyal user base who returns again and again. On the other hand, a great product with poor brand identity and strategy will likely be misunderstood or initially overlooked by its target demographic. Developing and curating your brand experience and story is an ongoing vocation with unpredictable twists and turns you'll have to adapt to. This might sound terrifying—you little control freak, you—but you do have control over a few things in this equation:

1. **Be Clear:** Find what your company is good at, find out who you can add benefit to, and tell that story in a way that is individual to you. Don't oversell, don't over-promise, don't bury the lead. Set honest expectations for what you can uniquely do in your industry.

2. **Deliver:** Do the work you said you could, and do it well. Consistently provide an experience that positively reflects your brand story.

If you can do these two things, your clients will respond with positive emotions, praise, repeat business, and social sharing. If you don't deliver, your clients will respond in turn, complaining to you and anyone who will listen online. They'll stop using your services.

Let's look at an example: Cafe du Monde in New Orleans. They only sell three things: beignets, coffee and milk. Daily, there's a snaking line well down Decatur Street, full of people waiting to get in. On the walls and on every table, they post their limited menu. People don't complain about the lack of options. Rather, the cafe has become world famous for making the most delicious beignets since 1862. They claim to do one thing and one thing well. And boy do they deliver on that promise. Be honest about what you do and own it.

The world is made up of humans—and humans, at their core, are just big balls of emotion. Most decisions made in this world, are not arrived upon through rational, analytical reasoning, but through feelings and emotions (rightly or wrongly). This is why it's so important to create a connection between your brand and your audience that goes beyond just buying and selling. Can you relate on an emotional level? It's the brand values and culture that often build the strongest loyalty.

Don't mistake the above advice to mean that you should be a pandering, people-pleaser, chasing potential customers around like a politician chasing votes, rattling off whatever sentiment you think they want to hear. Some of the most successful innovators went against the status quo to create something the world didn't even know it wanted or needed. Learn about your clients and audience, discover their goals and needs, understand their cultural situation, and then meet those needs in a way that leaves both you and them satisfied.

In his research on what makes an iconic brand, Douglas B. Holt unveils the concept of Cultural Branding. These brands read the cultural pulse of their audience, and appeal to that in a way that makes their products or services socially relevant. This makes the connection between brand and user more than just emotional, but relevant and real. It's more than just a brand proposition statement that defines why the brand's service is superior. It tells a story (a myth, Holt calls it) of why the brand is in tune with the human experience. This kind of connection with your user base is how your brand becomes something that is remembered, valued, and even championed by your customer. In order to stay relevant in this way, you have to continually adapt to an ever-changing human experience.

> *"In cultural branding, communications are the center of customer value. Customers buy the product to experience these stories. The product is simply a conduit through which customers can experience the stories that the brand tells. When consumers sip a Coke, Corona, or Snapple, they are drinking more than a beverage. Rather, they are imbibing identity myths anchored in these drinks. An effective cultural strategy creates a storied product, that is, a product that has distinctive branded features (mark, design, etc.) through which customers experience identity myths."*
>
> *How Brands Become Icons* by Douglas B. Holt.
> Copyright 2004 Harvard Business School Publishing Corporation; All Rights Reserved.

With this in mind, consider what emotions you want associated with your brand before working out what your brand identity looks like. Work out how you can connect with a consumer to improve their life. Work out how you can appeal to your consumer as a human, addressing their concerns with something that engenders trust. Then, work out what traditional or unique means you can use to visually and verbally transform yourself from being a stranger to being a friend. What's your road in? This isn't a pickup line at the bar or a "like" on Instagram, it's small talk at the grocery store or helping someone pick up the books they've dropped (oldest trick in the Rom-Com book). Just don't forget to follow through with actions that validate the initial impression. The most important question you can ask at the outset is, "Why?" Besides making money, why are you starting your business and brand?

Quiz: Getting to Know Your Brand

Ask yourself the following questions about your brand. Some might sound a bit repetitive from the business plan we made, and that's OK. You'll be meditating on the who, what and why of your brand often. Your answers will give you insight into who your brand could be, what it could look like, who you might appeal to, and how it could make a difference. Some questions might sound odd, but we're trying to imagine your brand's personality. The best stories are character-driven, and brand stories are no different.

1. Why do you exist (origin story of your company)?

2. Why should people care (what problem do you solve)?

3. Why do you care (your values, vision, and mission)?

4. Why you and not someone else (your competitive edge)?

5. If you had a celebrity spokesperson, who would it be?

6. If you had a theme song what would it be (or what genre of music)?

7. What is your patronus (the animal that best represents you)?

8. Describe your personality in 2 words. (Examples: clever, fun, warm, courageous, frank...)

9. Describe how you do business in 2 words. (Examples: efficient, inventive, reliable, adaptable...)

10. What are your hobbies?

11. Who are your dream clients and why would they enjoy your brand?

12. Why might people underestimate you? What is your weakness, and how could you jump that hurdle visually and verbally, turning those shortcomings into perceived strengths?

13. What is oddly awesome about you? Think about strange quirks and interests.

Done? Now, stress test what you just wrote. Compare them back to the research you gathered for your Business Plan, and then go a bit further. Do some online research about your industry and competition, talk to people in your industry, and talk to people who fit your client demographic: Is there a demand for the kind of brand you are describing? Do similar brands exist? Is the market overly saturated with similar brands or is there a hole there you can fill? How will the audience differentiate you from other companies? Find brands who are doing what you want to do or something similar and analyze their strengths and weaknesses. Find brands with similar goals and visions and dig into how they tell their story. Do all their identity systems look similar?

Do all their about statements sound the same? In what way can you stand out from the trend among them? Look for how you can learn from them and how you can deviate from them. Look at what type of client work they are mainly getting. Look at brands that are poorly managed and try and isolate where they fail. Make note of how you can avoid similar pitfalls. All of this mind-bending research will give you some direction on what styles, imagery, language and tactics you can use to help define your brand's identity and give it a unique advantage in the market.

The 10% You Can See: Brand Identity

We've covered the heart and soul of branding, so here's the skin and bones of it: the identity system. The identity system is the set of visual and verbal assets that give style to the substance of your brand. Here's some ideas on how to develop your staple identity assets.

Company Name

Here are some things to consider when choosing your business name:

1. **Availability:** Check that your choice of business name hasn't already been used by someone else (especially if they've trademarked it). Use the U.S. Patent and Trademark Office's online trademark search tool to see if a similar name, or variation of it, is trademarked. Trademark infringement can put a costly damper on your start-up hopes and dreams.

2. **Originality:** Try and find a name that is unique, but not too complex to remember, say, or spell. We perhaps failed this test on our company name. We grew up in upstate New York where Yiddish was commonly used by many. Chutzpah was a common term in our vocabulary. Fast forward 15 years later. We moved back to California, were in the midst of starting our new design business, and were toying with business names. Oh how clever we thought ourselves when we realized our last name, Hood, fit right into one of our favorite Yiddish words, chutzpah, which means to be bold, unapologetic, and brazen. Being the maximalists that we were, this word perfectly described our aesthetic and business approach. We mixed our name into the word and Hoodzpah was born. Unfortunately, a good portion of the rest of the country (and world) is not familiar with the Yiddish term. Not only that, but it's a hard word to pronounce and a harder word to spell since, technically, it's a remix of the original word. At this stage in our career, it's served as much as a talking point as it has as a hindrance, and we're glad to have it. Still, it does prove a hassle to spell over the phone to tech support and new clients. Silver lining? It makes SEO rankings a breeze.

3. **A Deeper Meaning:** Does the name tell a story? Does it have meaning that can help explain the "why" behind your business's unique approach and skill

set? For example, legend has it that Steve Jobs chose the name Apple, because he wanted people to start seeing computers as something universal, elementary and approachable, not something that only hobbyists enjoyed because it was complicated and niche. Few things are as disarming and simple as an apple. Even if that gets proven false, it's a lovely myth and paints our perfect example. Apologies for the cliché Apple references.

4. **Creating Your Own Meaning:** A made-up business name might be meaningless without context, but it should at least evoke a feeling that will align with your business as a brand. For example, "doinkus" is a fun made-up word to say, but the sound of it infers putziness and ridiculousness. Try and choose a made-up word that feels in-line with your services and brand personality. Need inspiration? Try www.Wordoid.com. This website will help you mishmash new words together based on your favorite letters and preferred length.

5. **Clarity:** Does the name create confusion about what you do? Using a name that doesn't directly apply to what you do is alright unless it creates brand confusion. Naming yourself "Tasty Treats" might seem like a quaint way to say you do delicious designs, but might also make people think you sell cupcakes or run a recipe blog. With enough marketing and messaging to contextualize, any name can be explained. Just ask yourself if you're willing to run that uphill road.

6. **Social Media:** Is the name available on social media and for domain purchase? Made up names that have good sound to them can be easier to lock down on social. If your business name is already taken, try adding descriptor words (example: "Barnaby" might be taken, but "BarnabyDesign" might be available). The goal is to keep it short and memorable so you can tell it to someone verbally. Also, getting the same handle across all social media platforms is hugely helpful when telling people how to find you, as they only need to remember one handle rather than five unique ones.

7. **Aesthetics:** Do the letter forms in the name appeal to you? Would they lend themselves to an interesting logo design or wordmark? Choosing a name that has meaning and is also visually appealing is quite a triumph.

Company Tagline

The tagline is a great place to build on your brand theme or story. It can also serve to give more pertinent information about your skills and offering. Beware of unintelligible or overly obscure tag lines. If your company name is a made-up or unfamiliar, use the tagline to help people understand what you do or why you do it.

Logo

Designing for yourself can be daunting. We are our own worst clients. You'll probably spend way too much time staring at a blank Illustrator screen thinking of logo concepts, and waste more than a few hours sweating, drinking, or crying over dead ends in the process. Try not to put too much stress on yourself (easier said than done). Yes, your logo should allude to your business's personality and values, but in no way will it tell the whole story. So don't be so precious about it that you seriously delay getting your business started. Aim for a good solution, not a perfect one, otherwise you'll never be done. Worst case scenario, you do your damnedest and find something that works for now, then change it up in a year when you've learned more about your business and brand culture.

The best you can do is treat this job like you would a client's. Do a proper discovery phase (which we luckily already did with our business plan and the quiz in this chapter), sketch concepts, put pen tool to artboard, and create your designs. Seek critique and feedback on your logo concepts from mentors and trusted peers. Once you're happy with it, develop a set of guidelines for fonts, colors, and other treatments you'll use throughout your identity system. Then let the animal out of its cage so you can see how it evolves naturally as you start applying it to designed pieces. If you're getting really stuck on your logo, don't underestimate the power of a good font. Set your company name in a quality font that reflects your company personality and style.

Your logo should be unique enough to be memorable, but simple enough to be able to morph and grow with the changing times. Practically speaking, it should also scale down or up easily. Consider how it will adapt from its smallest state (a favicon in someone's web browser), to its largest state. The logo doesn't have to stay the same in every usage scenario. Create variations of it for the different applications you might encounter down the road: a version with the icon only, a version with the wordmark only, a lockup with just the tagline, etc.. Have all of these variations saved and ready for print, web, or reverse white use. Here are some more tips when designing your logo:

1. **Classy beats trendy every time.** You need your branding to be inclusive, not exclusive. Think of your logo as your outfit on the first day of school. If it's too new, people think you're trying too hard and you might end up as the idiot who left the 32W x 34L sticker running down the leg of your Levis. Rather, go with the outfit you know works. You've gotten great feedback on it before. It makes you look good. It hugs all the right parts. It's current without being try hard. It's definitively you. Timeless style never fades, while a purely trendy look will date you sooner than you can say "stonewashed jeans." Try to find a median between your unique, cutting-edge style and a timeless *je ne sais quoi* that will keep your brand looking fresh, despite the latest fads.

2. **Consider the clients you will have in the short term as well as your dream clients.** Create a logo that could appeal to both if you can. Think of the connotations of everything before making a final decision on your logo design. Research cultural perceptions of your icon or color. At first you might think it's a great idea to use a butterfly icon in your design because it's your favorite creature and it's your favorite album by Mariah Carey. Now, sit back and play Barbara Walters. Let the overanalyzing begin. What might your butterfly icon communicate to the woman looking for a logo for her law firm? Well, it might make her think you are too juvenile in your style, or it might just remind her of the tramp stamp she got one wild night in Cabo. Either

way, not so great. There's no fool proof style that will be the catch-all of glory for all potential clients, but it is worth considering what every font, color, symbol, and motif says about what your business can or can't do.

3. **Make sure it's unique to you.** Once you've come up with a concept, if you're worried someone else might have already made a similar mark, reverse image search it on Google to be sure. Ask your lawyer to help you research and avoid any conflicting marks. You want a truly unique mark that you can eventually trademark. Also, try and avoid common themes already present in the market. Are a lot of design agencies using a similar aesthetic? Don't get lost in the noise, find your own melody.

Messaging and Voice

"Writing?! About myself and my company? Oh the horror! I'm a creative, not a novelist. I make pictures. I always lose at Scrabble. I'm not wired that way!"

Calm the cuss down.

Writing is a four-letter word to many creatives (well, except writers... *obviously*) and it shouldn't be. As a freelancer, business owner and the promoter of your brand, you have to know how to write. Let us rephrase that. As anyone who plans on making any sort of impact on a broader audience, you have to know how to write. We don't know who's perpetuating this persona about writing, like it's some mystic skill that only the chosen few can harness. It's not a level of nirvana. You're not threading a needle, or trying to fold a fitted sheet. As foreign as you think writing is, it's really not that far from what you do everyday. When you talk to your friends, when you persuade your partner to watch *Die Hard* instead of *Sleepless in Seattle*, when you try for the millionth time to explain to your mother "what exactly you're doing with your life" as a creative (yes, Mom, design is a valid career path). Every time you use words to persuade a client, explain a proof, or connect with someone, you are exercising the chops it takes to be a great writer.

What makes an epic writer is not grammar or sentence structure or even spelling (there are color coded squiggly lines in every word processing program for those). What makes a great writer is being able to communicate to your audience in a way that they can understand and relate to. Stop thinking of writing as that stapled five-paragraph essay you were trained to spew out for history class. Start thinking about it as a way to record a conversation for a future listener. You've got to get over the unmerited fear of writing. If you can learn to love/accept/deal with it, you'll be rewarded over and over again in the future. Writing proposals and emails will get simpler and less daunting. You'll be able to better explain your proofs with annotations. You'll be able to win over clients better. You'll be able to connect with potential clients online through blogs and portfolio blurbs. Your overall efficiency will go up, too. Here's some tips on how to tackle writing about yourself and your brand:

1. **Go into writing with a goal.** Have you ever started writing something only to find yourself completely lost on five different tangents two hours later? That's because you

went into the project without a clear goal to check your progress against. When you start, have a concise purpose. Make a bullet point outline. What's the main reason you're writing? Isolate that. Then bullet point the facts you want to include to support its key purpose. This will help you stay on track as you move on.

2. **Have a process.** If you get stage fright when you sit down to a blank screen on your computer, then find a process that helps you jump that white-page hurdle. Our process usually looks like this:

Step 1: Grab a piece of paper or open a blank Google Doc. At the top, simply write the main goal for the writing project. Then, quickly list rough ideas that need to be covered in the writing. It's basically a quick checklist of what you want to include. Not having to worry about complete sentences and witty phrasing will help you to just begin with the facts. Knowing what you need to say is half the battle.

Step 2: Organize those rough notes and ideas into sections. Maybe the bullet points end up being divided into three sections: the problem, the solution, and why it matters. Make sections that work for your purpose and gather your thoughts within them. Remove duplicate bullets or anything that now seems unnecessary.

Step 3: Now, organize these sections into a flow that better leads the reader through the story or process. Usually, you've already written your notes in the most organic way that makes sense to you, but it doesn't hurt to reread and reorganize with fresh eyes.

Step 4: You have your bullet points sectioned in the right order, now you need to make them into more polished sentences. Keep your sentences simple and to the point.

Step 5: Review the whole document again to add final personality touches and check for spelling, grammar, and the inevitable run-on sentence. When reading, make sure your original purpose still shines clearly, even with all that fleshy content.

3. **Be genuine.** Why are you trying to talk like Batman's butler? Why are you writing like an instructional manual reads? Beefing up on unnecessary technical language just muddies the waters. Be you. Just speak about what you know in the terms you and your target audience are familiar with. Explain why you care. Being genuinely passionate about what you do and why you do it will come through in your writing. The last thing you want to do is pretend you are something you aren't, getting caught by someone who does know the difference. You also don't want to come off like a condescending prick. What you do want to sound like is an excited, talented person who loves what they do. It's the reason that everyone loves Neil deGrasse Tyson: he takes very complex subjects and explains them in simple terms with pop-culture analogies that make it easy to digest.

4. **Choose your words carefully.** As you start writing about yourself and your work, you should work on developing a voice for your brand. Just like a person, every brand

has a unique tone and voice. When you talk about your brand on your website, what kind of language will you use? When you tweet to followers and reply to comments on your Facebook page, what is the tone of the communication? If you're a naturally funny person and feel your humor reflects your brand's values and message well, that might be a great voice to channel. If you aren't naturally funny, don't try to be. If you are looking to convey a more professional, reliable personality, don't use internet slang or cuss. If you want to be perceived as a more casual, laid back brand, loosen up with your language (just tread carefully). Consider words you want to associate with your brand, and words you want to avoid. Develop a voice that flows naturally for you and works for your audience. Above all else, be considerate. Whatever your voice, you don't want to write in a way that offends or insults your audience.

5. **Have ready-made content.** Once you've worked out what you want to say about your company, how you want to say it, and to whom. Gather the following pieces together in a folder that's easy to find. If you are ever interviewed by a podcast, blog, or magazine, or you give a keynote at a conference or a school, they will need this info and it's easier to have it ready on hand.

    a. **Your Company Bio:** one or two paragraphs is fine.

    b. **Your Value Proposition Statement:** A succinct synopsis (one to two sentences) of the above paragraph. This is the 30-second pitch for when you see Mark Cuban or Barbara Corcoran on the moving walkway at DFW airport. You've got to pitch yourself fast.

    c. **Your Service List:** Name your services and give a brief explanation of what they are and why they are valuable to clients.

    Keep these assets in a master document. Having these things thoughtfully written out in your desired voice and tone, spell-checked, and ready for action, will save you time and effort when you get ready to build your website and social media profiles. Winging it every time you create a new account is exhausting and leads to profiles riddled with errors or slapped together information that doesn't best embody your business's brand.

For those of you still not sold on writing, or who can't find the time to do it well, hire a freelancer or a clever friend to help you out with these messaging assets. Give the writer the bullet points on what you want to say, explain the desired tone, and let them do their magic.

Brand Guidelines

After you've settled on your logo and core messaging, put together a simple brand guideline for yourself. The goal is to begin creating a recognizable and cohesive aesthetic for your brand. A happy side-effect of defining these terms is that it makes designing collateral for your business much more efficient in the future. Brand guidelines can include:

1. **Core brand fonts.** Establish what will be your display header fonts, what will be used for body copy, etc.. Try to keep the number of fonts you use to a minimum. Too many fonts in all sorts of styles gets cluttered. Think of legibility and compatibility with the logo.

2. **Brand colors.** Define the Pantone color, RGB, CMYK, and hex code for each color in your brand color palette so you can easily access it when needed.

3. **Do's and Don'ts:** if you never want someone to use your logo on a 45 degree angle, specify that! If the logo should never be used on a photo background, specify that. If the logo has requirements for the amount of clear space or padding that surround it, specify that. Besides being an exercise in defining the core visual pillars of your brand, the style guide also ensures that any designer who gets their hands on your logo and identity assets will know how to correctly apply them without you having to be there to walk them through it.

4. **Mission statement, value proposition statement, key messaging and brand tone :** We know, we know... we've talked on these ad nauseam. Add them to your brand guidelines, and think about adding a vocabulary list too. Words you do and don't want used when speaking about your brand.

Collateral

With all your messaging and logo assets at the ready, you'll want to create things like business cards, thank you cards, social media skins, and no doubt the ubiquitous rubber stamp with your logo on it. Work within a reasonable budget to create a professional, unified set of collateral that will help sell your company as a capable, exciting and professional outfit to prospective clients.

You can create a promotional piece that presents your messaging and qualifications in a compelling way. If you have great stats and testimonials about the power of your services for companies, include that. Provide case studies if you've got them. Make it easy to digest and very visual. This can be a great tool to send to prospective clients as a digital attachment or as a printed book. If you don't have work inquiries coming into your inbox, it's time to start reaching out to people for work.

Remain consistent when creating your identity system and collateral assets. Consider each piece as part of a whole, so that everything looks intentional and cohesive. If you're getting stuck, look for well-designed templates to get you started. Sites like www.CreativeMarket.com have a lot of reasonably priced design templates for brochures, business cards, client presentations, and more. If you're not a designer who is fluent in InDesign or Illustrator, you can still make layouts easily and beautifully using Google Docs and Google Slides, or any word processing app. Or trade a designer for your creative services (they likely need photography, or writing, or whatever you specialize in). Take pride in all your collateral and make it sing. These are your subtle commercials to clients, showing them what they should be doing with their own brand.

Your Brand Asset Folder

Collect the fonts, motifs, patterns, logo files, brand guidelines, and any other commonly used assets, and put them into a spot on your computer where you can find and access and use them easily. Do it. Seriously... right now. We'll wait.

The Website

Your website is one of the most powerful marketing assets in your tool chest. Acquiring jobs and clients hinges hugely on your website. You need a professional and current online hub where people can check out your work, learn about your process, check out your qualifications, and submit inquiries for projects. Invest in a legitimate domain name (www.JohnDoe.freesite.com doesn't cut it). You don't have to know how to code to get a great site on a budget. Wordpress (www.Wordpress.org) is an excellent content management platform for creatives who might not have the time, patience, or coding knowledge to create their own site. Through Wordpress themes you can easily install a ready-designed template. Most themes come with demo content that can be installed with one click. Then it's up to you to customize the information, graphics and images to suit your own needs. When searching for a theme for Wordpress, we recommend using www.Themeforest.net. They have a huge library by great developers and designers. Look for a Wordpress theme that has good ratings, a high number of purchases, is made by an Elite Author, is compatible with the most current Wordpress version, and is responsive or mobile-friendly. More and more people are accessing your site on their phones and tablets and you don't want their experience on your site to be cumbersome or unfriendly.

Wordpress is a free platform to install, and amazing themes are usually only a one-time fee of $40 to $60 on Themeforest. Plus, they allow for loads of customization. You can hire someone at www.Studio.Envato.com to do customizations that are more extensive in the code. You can even hire someone there to install your theme and import the demo content for you. Wordpress has a lot of amazing plugins that extend your theme's features even further. We use a great plugin called Yoast SEO to enable more SEO (Search Engine Optimization) options on our site. It helps us optimize our content and analyze the readability of our posts. With Wordpress's open-source flexibility comes a bit of vulnerability. Plugin and theme incompatibility issues can break your site, and updates to the Wordpress platform don't always jive with your unique setup. So be ready to invest in upkeep. This is a part of business. A website isn't a one-time investment. It will need to evolve with you and with technology. Set aside a fund for fixes and renovations. Think of it as your online store front. Even after you've bought the store, you'll need to clean it and spruce it up here and there. This is true no matter what web solution you choose.

Another great platform for creating a simple and cost-effective website is www.Squarespace.com. They have beautifully clean, responsive, minimal themes. The sites are easy to publish content to, they offer e-commerce solutions, they take care of your domain and hosting (with Wordpress you have to do this separately), they provide 24/7 support, and they only charge $12 to $40 a month to do so (as of writing this). Their solution is an ongoing subscription, unlike Wordpress, which mainly involves one-time fees. If you really don't want to be bothered with setting up the hosting and domain, building your own site, configuring SEO, and troubleshooting errors along the way, Squarespace is the easiest answer for your needs, albeit much less customizable in certain functionalities when compared to Wordpress. Later on, if you feel like switching to Wordpress, you can export your Squarespace website's content (not the styling, but the words and images) into a Wordpress compatible format. Sadly, you can't take their themes with you.

If you are determined to create a completely custom site but don't know how to code, trade with a web developer. Make a deal, sell a kidney, do whatever it takes to get a website that fits your branding, meets your online goals, and presents you as a professional. At the very least you should have a www.Dribbble.com or www.Behance.net profile that you keep updated.

Once you've created your site and filled it with your company bio, your "why" statement, your services, your portfolio and a contact form, be sure to update it regularly with current work that showcases your ever-growing talents and clients. Avoid putting up work that is clearly from a school project. It makes you look green. Don't have a blog on your site if you aren't going to post regularly to it. There's nothing worse than a website where the latest blog reads, "Welcome to Our New Site!" and is dated three years ago. It makes things look neglected and irrelevant.

Lifestyle Branding

Your company's appeal isn't defined by services and pricing alone. The modern creative landscape is an oversaturated market. Your potential clients are in a constant state of social, informational, and visual overload. Create something "extra" to convince them to choose you over the next person. People are looking for more. They are looking for personality, for something they can relate to, believe in. They want to see a creative firm with purpose, passion, conviction, and an aesthetic that inspires them or matches their own. They're looking for that human element. Or at least the ideal client is. If you're just competing for lowest price, you're inviting a specific type of client into your world. One that values bargain prices over quality and time. This can lead to a strained relationship if you're not aligned in that goal. The other risk you take: there's always someone willing to undercut your price. Trying to be the cheapest is a long walk off a short pier. It's a lot of work for a bleak reward. Instead, focus on your qualities that prove you're

*
HOODZPAH
HOT-TAKE

Trying to be the cheapest is a long walk off a short pier. It's a lot of work for a bleak reward.

worth more. Focus on painting a portrait of your company culture to create that human connection.

Think of it from your client's perspective: choosing a creative is like hiring a nanny. They're trusting you with their baby: their business. It's personal to them. They've labored growing it and tending to it. Now they're paying you out of their hard-earned dollars to take care of it. And they don't even know you. They're already jittery because they've heard horror stories of bad nannies. They're sceptical and wary. Help them over that hump. Go beyond the standard résumé and nice-looking website. Let people into your world. Reveal your brand's culture alignments and interests through great storytelling. It's sometimes referred to as lifestyle branding. At the very least, broad lifestyle branding can make you relatable as real people with real ideas, preferences and interests. More niche sub-culture lifestyle branding can help align you with likeminded people who identify with your company as a champion of their interests.

People want to believe in the products and services they purchase. When we started Hoodzpah, we learned this almost by accident. Living in Southern California, we are surrounded by lifestyle brands. The whole action sports industry is a giant lifestyle branding machine. Having watched surf and skate brands do this for years, it was second nature to adopt similar methods when we began branding and marketing our own company. We took the lifestyle we lived and loved everyday, and incorporated it into our design aesthetic and company's personality. We created content that projected our lifestyle and that attracted the kind of people we wanted to work with—people who enjoy culture, music, art, sports, and good design. We used our life experiences and interests as excuses to practice the design we wanted to be paid for.

For example, we have always been fascinated by Kustom Kulture and all things vintage. Countless hours have been spent scrounging through bins at Goodwill for Tom T. Hall records, combing flea markets for old Frye boots, swooning over chopper marvels at Born Free Motorcycle Show, or making the bi-monthly visit to the mechanic when Amy's '72 Mercedes is acting up. They say "write what you know" and we figured "draw what you know" was close enough. For fun, we began making vintage inspired posters. One of the extremely popular prints was of a motorcycle at Bonneville, with a dust cloud wake creating the silhouette of a woman's face. It was shown at Deus Ex Machina for the Oil & Ink Expo, a touring motorcycle-themed art show. We were exposed to a new audience who shared common interests. That piece opened the door to quality, paying work for us from people who aligned with our lifestyle.

Another example: early on, we shared our design process. We always wondered how other artists were working, but not many were willing to share their methods, tips, and tricks. In the spirit of engendering transparency, we got a decent camera and a 50mm lens and started documenting our projects and methodology. With the quality of phone cameras these days, you don't even need a professional camera to do this. We shared everything on Facebook, Twitter, Dribbble, Instagram, and our blog. We showed our audience the makers and process behind the company. Our audience engagement rose. Social media turned from a purely fun outlet for personal projects, into a place where we were garnering business and building a community that was genuinely invested in our brand culture.

We were building a reputation and our audience began to perceive us as people who understood design, style, story, and culture. This led to some interesting things:

1. Clients hired us to do "our style."

2. Clients hired us because we fit the target demographic they were looking to connect with.

This was when we started getting the clients that we wanted in the industries that we were interested in. Our investment in telling our story meant clients came to us with a sense that they knew us, before we ever met.

We aren't trying to host a reality show (if you're reading this, Andy Cohen, we *could* be persuaded if the price is right…), but we *are* trying to show snapshots of how we do things, why we do things, and who we are doing things with. Documenting interesting clients we design for, taking photos of friends who inspire us culturally and aesthetically, doing a behind the scenes video of our joint effort with a few friends to put together a drive-in movie theatre for Orange County (fun fact: one of said friends is Lindsey Bro, who edited this very book!), sharing our workday music playlists, taking photos of a new art piece one of us just finished – these are all fun ways we have tried to welcome our audience into our world. Peppering personal, funny, and culturally informative content in with our portfolio work makes our company real to people. Suddenly, we aren't just a faceless group of ambiguous creatives. It's like VH1's *Behind the Music*, but without the cocaine and only a fraction of the leather.

There's a caveat to lifestyle branding. If the lifestyle you lead is very niche, or is on the fringe, there's a chance that you could alienate future clients while appealing only to a sub section. Depending on the kind of work you want, this could be a win or loss. Ask yourself, is the story I'm revealing about my company's culture going to attract my ideal clients? Can the sub-culture I represent and appeal to afford my services? Do they even want my services? If not, then you might broaden you story a bit, or rethink your target audience. However if you value working on certain projects with certain people above what pay you might get, then perhaps weeding out uninterested demographics suits your goals.

Chapter Checklist: To Do

- ☐ Finalize your business name.
- ☐ Create your logo and tagline. Save final file variations.
- ☐ Create a simple brand guidelines book and save a brand assets folder.
- ☐ Create the collateral pieces you need to get started, i.e. business cards, promotional deck, social media shareables and cover photos, etc..

- [ ] Get a portfolio site up, either on your own domain or through one of the portfolio sites mentioned.

- [ ] Write a list of interests that you and your dream clients share. What are your common cultural influences? How can you weave that inspiration and backstory into your own brand story to highlight shared experience and familiarity?

- [ ] Create a side project based on something that interests you (as well as interests others). These kinds of projects are more likely to grow wings when the topic is relatable. Bring on a creative friend to make it more exciting (while also growing the shared audience). Need some ideas? Here you go:

    a. Re-imagine or pay homage to your favorite albums, movies or books. 10x is a great example. 10x is a yearly design challenge curated by Eric R. Mortensen and Skinny Ships where 20 to 30 artists are invited to re-design the album art for their 10 favorite music albums for that year. Check 2018's lineup at www.10x18.co. Whatever the theme, hashtag and tag the artist, TV show, or movie to make sure the right audience can find your work.

    b. Give yourself a creative challenge once a day or once a week, depending on how much free time you have. Lists exist to prompt you on these challenges. There's the Daily UI Challenge, the Daily Logo Challenge, Inktober, 36 Days of Type. Choose a creative vein, then find a challenge to participate in. Most importantly, share the process. Document it and tag official accounts organizing or publicising it. You could make your own, but why not participate in the community already doing it? There's built-in audience and visibility.

*Yet another blank page in case
you want to tear out the poster
on the next page.*

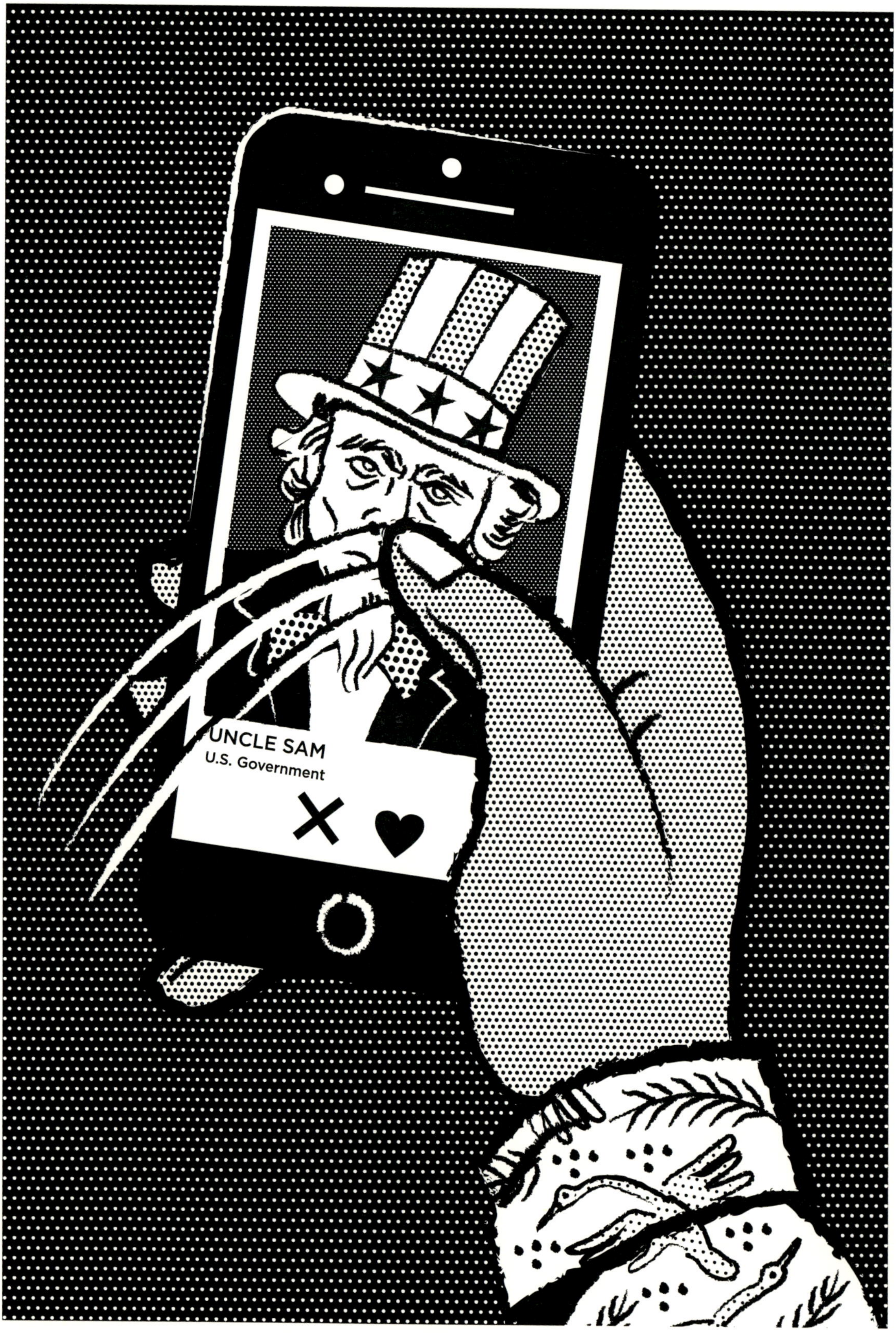

Illustration by Amy Hood of Hoodzpah (Hoodzpahdesign.com)

7
Making It Official

*It's time to put
this dream on the books.*

———

Everyone hates an all-talk-no-action guy/gal, so gosh darn it, let's make things official. In order to register your business with Uncle Sam you need to decide what type of business you will set up. Will you register as a sole proprietorship, partnership, corporation, or Limited Liability Company (LLC)? *Errr...what's the difference?* Glad you asked.

Choosing the Right Business Structure

Below is a rundown of the most common small business types for freelancers and small businesses in the United States, and a list of pros and cons for each. You'll need to know what kind of business you are before you can setup a bank account, do your taxes, or even file for a DBA (Doing Business As). Review the options below, and ask your accountant or lawyer for further advice before filing paperwork (especially if you are from somewhere other than the U.S., as your options will vary). As you grow your business, you can change your business structure to suit your changing needs.

Along with the definition of each business structure in the following pages, we've included a link to the Small Business Administration's website for info on what forms and steps are required for that specific business type. The particulars can vary per state, and the SBA (Small Business Association) site will help you know what's needed for your location. Your accountant can help you prepare and file these documents. For the simpler structures, you can often handle the paperwork on your own, and save some cash. Once you choose your structure and file your forms, you've established a company!

Sole Proprietorship

> *"A sole proprietorship is the simplest and most common structure chosen to start a business. It is an unincorporated business owned and run by one individual with no distinction between the business and you, the owner. You are entitled to all profits and are responsible for all your business's debts, losses and liabilities."*
>
> - Small Business Association (www.SBA.gov).

The great thing about being a sole proprietor is that you don't have to file any forms to officially be one. However, you might need a license or permit in order to operate. Skip ahead to the "Obtain Licenses and Permits" section of this chapter to find out which ones you need.

YAY! IT'S THE EASIEST AND CHEAPEST BUSINESS STRUCTURE TO ESTABLISH.

The cost to start a sole proprietorship totals whatever your license and permit fees are. Tax prep is simple and, as a sole proprietorship, your business is not taxed separate from you as an individual. Just file once as yourself, using your social security number. Of all the business structures, these are the lowest tax rates you'll find.

BUMMER. YOU'RE LIABLE AND YOU HAVE TO PAY THE SELF-EMPLOYMENT TAX.

Because you are technically considered one with your business, you are personally liable for any debts owed by your business. This includes liabilities caused by your employees' actions. Be aware that your personal property can be seized for debts. You also have to pay the self-employment tax. This is pretty much the combined Social Security and Medicare tax that an employer would normally pay half of. You'd see this as the FICA tax on any pay stub from an employer if you worked for someone. Except you are your own employer, so you have to pay the whole thing.

According to the IRS website (www.IRS.gov), for self-employment income earned, the self-employment tax rate is currently (as of 2016) 15.3%. This rate consists of two parts: 12.4% for social security (old-age, survivors, and disability insurance) and 2.9% for Medicare (hospital insurance). You'll pay 15.3% on the first $118,500 you make and then 2.9% on everything above that (per year). Be sure to check on the most current rates.

Partnership

A simple business structure that caters to a business with more than one owner. While there are a few different kinds of partnerships, they all have the same goal:

> "A Partnership is the relationship existing between two or more persons who join to carry on a trade or business. Each person contributes money, property, labor or skill, and expects to share in the profits and losses of the business."
>
> - IRS (www.IRS.gov).

For information on the steps and documents needed to officially form a partnership, visit www.SBA.gov/content/partnership.

YAY! GENERAL PARTNERSHIPS ARE EASY AND CHEAP TO SETUP, PLUS YOU HAVE SOMEONE ELSE CONTRIBUTING TO THE BUSINESS WITH YOU.

The cost to start a general partnership totals the fees associated with your licenses and permits. Depending on your allocation of responsibility, you also have someone to share in the financial commitments and growth of the business. Generally speaking, the more money, talent, hats and connections are thrown in the kip, the quicker things seem to get off the ground. Wisely chosen partners mean more good ideas, more marketable skills, and a larger existing network to draw upon for new clients.

The most important part of forming a partnership is coming up with your Partnership Agreement. This document outlines boundaries, ownership percentages, and partner roles (this is especially helpful at the beginning). It might seem formal, but it's a great stress-test for your business relationship. If you can't see eye to eye on the basic pillars of an agreement, then you should reconsider the partnership or choice of partner.

You can find great Partnership Agreement templates online to customize and make them your own. Start with their outline and then go through line by line and tailor it to your particular needs. Using a template helps save money on a lawyer initially, but it's highly recommended you get your final draft reviewed by a lawyer. You want to be certain everyone is protected and that you haven't missed any blaring loopholes. At the very least, make sure your agreement covers:

- Ownership percentages
- Profit and loss allocation
- Salaries
- Decision-making procedures and any hierarchy
- Exit strategies
- Roles and responsibilities.

BUMMER. YOU'RE LIABLE. WITH MORE THAN ONE PERSON IN CHARGE, THERE'S ALWAYS THE POTENTIAL FOR CONFLICTING OPINIONS. OH, AND YOU HAVE TO SHARE THE REVENUE.

Like a sole proprietorship, a general partnership holds you personally liable for any debts owed by your business. This applies to any of your partner's actions as much as your own. Remember, they're taking a risk on you, too. Your personal property can be seized to cover debts (even ones your partner is responsible for).

With partners, you might disagree about how you want to run the show or grow the party. Maybe they're more of a quiet-night-at-home-playing-Settlers-of-Catan kind of person and you're more of a head-to-Joshua-Tree-with-nothing-but-a-coffee-can-full-of-peyote kind of person. You have to find your common ground and meet in the middle. It's imperative you learn how to communicate effectively, figuring out the best way you can work together.

Last, you need to share everything you make (depending on the terms of your agreement, of course). To keep things not weird, let your agreement outline how profits are shared. You might be saying to yourself "I'd never let money get between my partnership," or "My partner would never screw me over" and we hope that's true. But you'd be a fool not to prepare and protect yourself by considering and outlining policies for every possible "what if" scenario, because money—or the feeling of a lack thereof—makes humans do strange things.

Limited Liability Company (LLC)

An LLC is a mix between a Partnership (or Sole Proprietor structure) and the more complicated Corporation structure. This still has your business income taxed as personal income, but you get the benefits of limited liability (meaning you aren't personally responsible for debts or legal claims against your business). For more information on this business structure and it's forms and requirements, visit www.SBA.gov/content/limited-liability-company-llc.

YAY! YOU HAVE LIMITED LIABILITY AND THERE'S MORE OPERATIONAL FLEXIBILITY.

In an LLC, you can be protected from some or all of your liability. Compared to an S-Corporation, you have less registration paperwork, but similar start-up costs. Profit sharing is also less restricted than other structures. Flow-through income taxation is simple to account for. There are no ownership restrictions and you can structure management however you want. The lifespan of the company can continue even if a member leaves or dies (in most states).

BUMMER. THERE'S A LITTLE MORE INVOLVED IN FORMING ONE, AND YOU NEED TO PAY SELF-EMPLOYMENT TAXES.

States require you to file Articles of Organization and draft an Operating Agreement to form an LLC. While this is not as extensive as what you have to create to form a corporation, it's still more involved than the automatic status of being a sole proprietor. Like a sole proprietor, LLC managing members also have to pay self-employment taxes (see sole proprietor section for an explanation of this).

Corporation (S or C)

A corporation is a more complex business structure with many more ongoing requirements. The C corporation is the standard corporation, and the S corporation has a special tax status with the IRS. The biggest difference between an S and C corporation type is in the way they are taxed. C corps are separately taxable entities that have to file and pay their own taxes, while S corporations are pass-through tax entities that don't have to pay their own income tax. Pass-through means that the S corps profit/loss is reported on the owners' personal tax returns and paid at the individual level. Another main difference is that an S corp has ownership limitations. There can be no more than 100 shareholder/owners, shareholders must be U.S. citizens/residents, and shareholders cannot be C corporations, other S corporations, LLCs, partnerships or many trusts. On the other hand, a C corp has no restrictions on ownership. For information on what steps and documents are needed to officially form a corporation, visit www.SBA.gov/content/corporation.

YAY! YOU HAVE LIMITED LIABILITY AND BETTER LONGTERM OPTIONS.

Both S corps and C corps offer limited liability protection to business owners (or shareholders), and can continue to exist even if ownership or management changes. Sole proprietorship and partnerships (and also LLCs in some states) end if an owner leaves or dies. A corporation also lets you transfer your share of ownership in the company easily, unlike partnerships or proprietorships. It's as simple as endorsing and signing over your stock certificates that represent your share of the company. This attribute can make your company more appealing to investors, who you can easily transfer shares to. Most would agree that corporations are the best structure for eventual public companies.

BUMMER. IT'S MORE EXPENSIVE TO FORM, THERE'S MORE PAPER WORK AND OBLIGATIONS, AND POTENTIAL FOR MORE TAX BURDEN.

The work involved in incorporating is very extensive, and best done by a professional. It can cost between $500 and $1500. S and C corps require extensive articles of incorporation to be filed with the state. Both also require ongoing corporate obligations like issuing stock, adopting bylaws, holding shareholder meetings, filing annual reports, and paying annual fees. If the rules of incorporation aren't followed, a court could pierce the corporate veil of protection and hold owners personally liable. Sometimes your tax burden will increase when you incorporate, and double taxation can occur.

Which business structure is right for you?

Corporations and LLCs (the incorporation options) are more advanced business structures that might not be the best investment of your money at the beginning. You can likely get by as a partnership or sole proprietor to save time and money while you prove your business model. Consider incorporating when your business liabilities and income grow to the point that you want to protect your personal assets by separating them from your company's. For the best advice, ask your CPA or business lawyer.

Rules and Regulations for Starting a Small Business

You've chosen your business structure and you've filed all the forms associated with that decision. Since you're now a legal business, it's time to introduce yourself to the government.

The U.S. Small Business Association (SBA) is an independent agency of the federal government of the United States of America, created in 1953 to "aid, counsel, assist and protect" small business concerns. According to the SBA, you must take the following steps for the government to consider you a legitimate business.

Obtain Licenses and Permits

Before you start manhandling projects, it's best to get the regulatory hullabaloo over with. Depending on your city, county and state, you'll need a number of particular licenses and permits. The requirements vary so contact your town/city clerk first. They can tell you about local requirements and hopefully advise on who to contact for state requirements. If you live in another country, talk to the small business section of your government about requirements. Google should lead you there easily. Just be patient and diligent, even if the government doesn't feel like the model of efficiency. Expect some frustration along the way and prepare yourself for the static-y, soft rock hold music.

In addition to your licenses and permits, you also need a Tax Identification Number (TIN). This number is associated with your business and you'll use it when filing taxes. Your TIN will either be an Employer Identification Number (EIN) you apply for with the IRS, or your existing Social Security Number. Usually, you'll find yourself applying for that EIN.

ACCORDING TO THE IRS, YOU NEED AN EIN IF ANY OF THE FOLLOWING APPLY:

- Your business has employees
- You operate your business as a Corporation or a Partnership
- You file any of these tax returns: Employment, Excise, or Alcohol, Tobacco and Firearms
- You withhold taxes on income, other than wages, paid to a non-resident alien
- You have a Keogh plan (a tax deferred pension plan available to self-employed people or unincorporated businesses for retirement purposes).

If none of the above are you, you can use your Social Security Number as your Tax ID when filing. Visit www.IRS.gov for more information and to apply for an EIN.

After you've worked out your Federal Tax Identification Number, check if your state requires a state number or charter for filing taxes. This can usually be found on your state government's website. Again, if lost, consult Google search bar.

Register Your Business Name (DBA)

If you want to name your business anything other than your personal legal name or the legal name of your partnership/corporation, then you must register a "Doing Business As" (DBA) with your local government. For example, our legal partnership is called "Hoodzpah, Inc." so we have to file a DBA if we want to go by "Hoodzpah Design Co." instead.

Registering a DBA is either done at the County Clerk's Office or with the State Government, depending on your location. Take heed that a few states do not require registering a fictitious business name (or DBA).

ACCORDING TO THE SBA, A DBA IS NEEDED IN THE FOLLOWING SCENARIOS:

- Sole Proprietors or Partnerships: If you wish to start a business under anything other than your legal name, you'll need to register a DBA so that you can do business as another name.

- Existing Corporations or LLCs: If your business is already set up and you want to do business under a name other than your existing corporation or LLC name, you will need to register a DBA.

Get Familiar with Business Laws and Regulations that Apply to You:

This is where having a lawyer on your A-Team can be really handy. Ask if there are any laws or regulations you need to be careful to comply with. Reading legalese can really blow your hair back so visit www.SBA.gov and search "Understand Business Law" for a good time... or just ask your lawyer.

Chapter Checklist: To Do

- ☐ Choose your business structure.

- ☐ File for any licenses or permits required.

- ☐ Figure out what your Tax Identification Number (TIN) is for your business. Is it your Social Security Number? Or do you need to apply for an EIN through the IRS?

- ☐ Get a DBA / Fictitious Business Name if you are doing business under a name other than your personal legal name, or other than your business' legal name.

- ☐ Talk to your lawyer about ongoing obligations and ask about what laws you need to be keen on before you start conducting business.

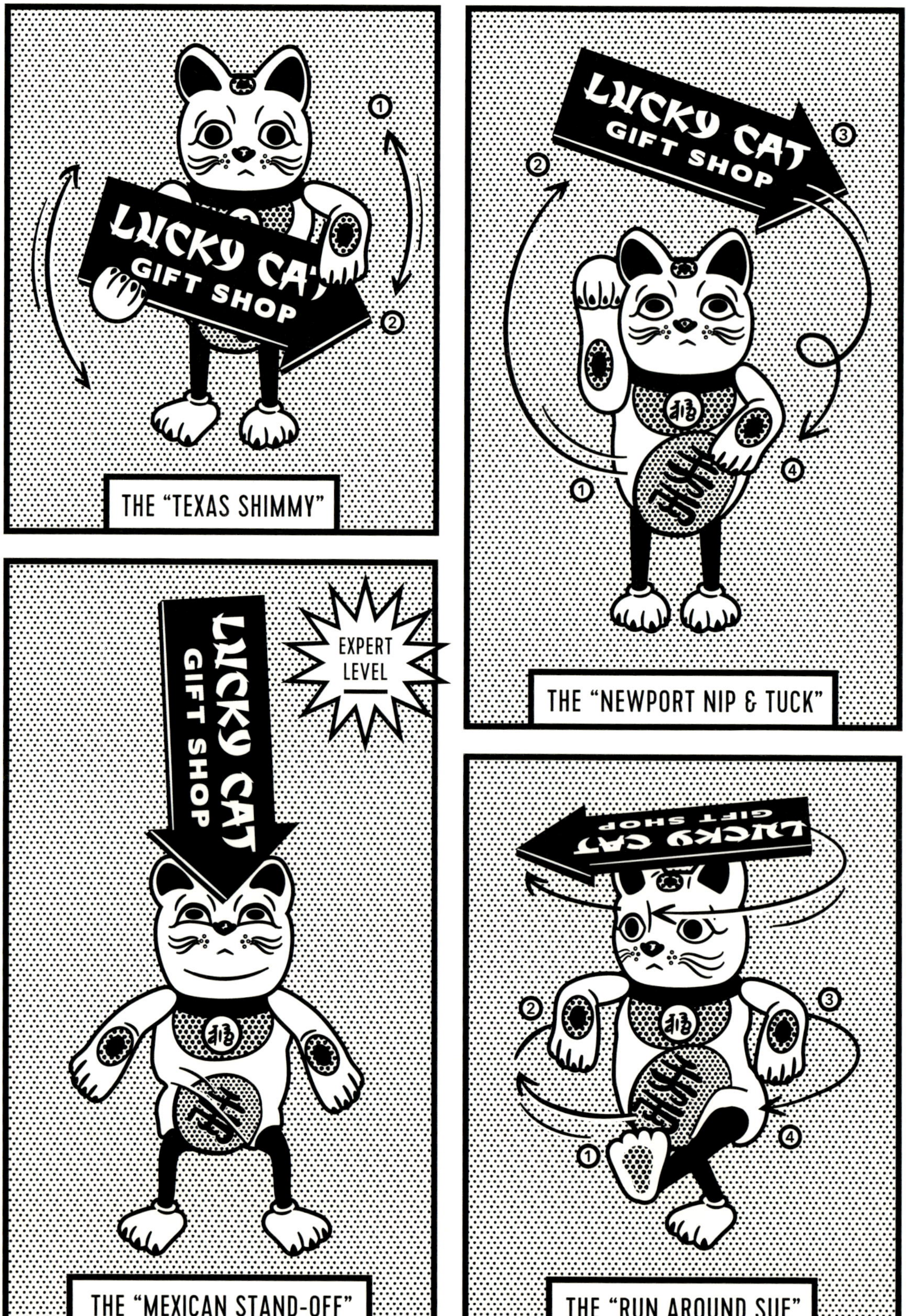

Illustration by Amy Hood of Hoodzpah

8

Growing Audience, Promoting Yourself, and Getting Work

Being your own hype guy, being your own Jock Jams track, being your own agent.

———

Let's just take a minute to congratulate ourselves. Go us! By going through these last chapters, you have already picked your company name, drafted your "About" statements, considered your company's purpose, created a cohesive and compelling logo and brand style (or at least you've started thinking about it), put together a company website to show off your shiny skills, acquired social media handles, and made your business official. You are already taking huge and positive steps as a small business owner! But what is a business without a patron? The "build it and they will come" method is not a very reliable one. Here are some tips to getting your business in front of potential clients. As usual, our goal is to suggest ways and means that are cheap and easy. You really can achieve a lot with a small budget and a "can do" attitude.

The Secret Sauce: People

HAPPY CLIENTS CAN DO YOUR BUSINESS DEVELOPMENT FOR YOU.

In the beginning, all of our jobs came to us via a friend, a friend-of-a-friend, or a recommendation from a former or current client. It's the easiest way to get work without paying for advertising. Plus, a referral from a real-life human has so much more return-on-investment (ROI) than any SEO, ad, or coupon. Be it good or bad, as a newbie at business, your first clients will likely be your friends and family. Many people warn against working with these exact groups, but in all reality, you have to start somewhere. If you can impress and deliver with these people, then they'll carry your banner to the ends of the earth. Same thing with happy clients. Everyone loves to be the person who has the right connection to refer their friends and family to.

Recommendations from personal acquaintances are the most trusted form of advertising, according to a 2015 Nielsen Global Online Consumer Survey of over 20,000 Internet consumers from 60 countries. Eighty-three percent of consumers surveyed noted that they trust word of mouth recommendations from people they know.

UNDERCOVER FUTURE CLIENTS ARE EVERYWHERE.

Remember that everyone you meet in life could be a potential client. We're not saying to be a car salesman all the time; but be aware of how you treat people in general. You are your brand to some extent, in that you are the face of your company and a key factor in your brand experience. Remember this when you're out and about in your daily life. Don't be rude, don't be flaky, and don't use more cusses than conjunctions in casual conversation. The most mundane of conversations can come back to bite you in the butt if you're not careful. If you go on a tirade about the shortcomings of your current client to a new acquaintance, they will remember that. And those anger management issues might make them think twice about potentially hiring you for a project. A good tip overall: be a decent human.

BE ON THE BALL.

Respond to new work inquiries promptly. Research shows that 35-50% of sales go to the vendor that responds first. (Source: www.InsideSales.com)

REMIND PEOPLE THAT YOU EXIST.

The best advice we can give you for earning clients organically with minimal cash investment is to just stay on your audience's radar and remind them you exist. It's easier to land work from people you already know or have already worked with. Post about your creative work regularly to your social media. Create unique gifts or promo pieces that showcase your skills, then give them to old clients or acquaintances you'd like to work with. Send out emails to clients and friends when you see something that reminds you of them. We actually have a lot of clients that we share music suggestions with regularly via Spotify. We have good enough relationships with some clients that we can text them when we see their product out and about, etc.

The goal here is to keep a line of communication open without a hard sales pitch. Interact with your clients via their social media. It'll make them look good and they will likely reciprocate, opening your reach up to their network too. Be tasteful, whatever you do. You don't have to send out a mass email or Facebook message begging for work, but there's also nothing wrong with announcing to your following that you're available for new projects or have openings in your upcoming schedule. It's all about how you phrase it. Don't come on too strong. Show your audience the awesome work you are doing and remind them that you are thinking of them.

TELL PEOPLE YOU EXIST AT ALL.

There's nothing wrong with reaching out to potential clients who don't know you yet. Research your dream clients. Then find people who work at those places (you can reverse look up employees at a company on LinkedIn). Follow those people on social and start interacting with them casually to build rapport (Twitter is an amazing place for this).

Does the company have a contact form on their site? Use it. Yes, this is a cold email. No, it won't kill you. Keep your message short and sweet. Let them know why you enjoy what they're doing, tell them about what you can offer if they need creative services, then link to your website so they can see your portfolio. For crying out loud link to your website or attach a web-optimized PDF. Ain't nobody got time to email you back to ask for what you should have logically thought to include. In short, you stand to lose nothing by reaching out, but you stand to lose a great potential client by doing nothing.

---

*

HOODZPAH HOT-TAKE

RE: COLD EMAILING

Make your email user-friendly. Meaning: Keep it short, include your services, and link your website or attach your web optimized portfolio pdf.

Attend events inside and outside of your industry to meet new people and widen your audience. Meeting new peers in the creative world (who could refer work to you or subcontract you) could be just as useful as meeting people in an industry different than yours (who could be your next client). Don't go into any social event with only sales on the brain. That's like going into a first date with wedding plans already in sight. You'll come off over eager and intense. Go in with the genuine goal of learning about people and making honest connections.

Getting Your Work Noticed Online

Use Dribbble, Behance, Medium, etc. as Springboards

Do you already have a Behance or Dribbble account? Fabulous! Those websites are well indexed, highly trafficked sites. Initially, people are much more likely to find your work on those websites than your own. So use those profiles as a launchpad. Link to your website from your profile. When posting on a recent project to these sites, leave out a few pictures and details. Then encourage visitors to go to your website for a full look at the project. Backlinks from high ranking websites like these will help boost your SEO ranking in the eyes of search engines like Google.

Create Quality Content About Your Industry and Work

Vlog on Youtube, story on Instagram, blog on your own site, or blog on a well trafficked site like www.Medium.com, and then encourage users to learn more about your process and work on your own site. Either way, the SEO benefits will show. Posting on your own site regularly will show search engines that you are an active site that consistently talks about certain keywords. Those keywords will likely be related to your field and your work, and that will help you get better ranking for those terms in the search engine's algorithm.

Use Free SEO Plugins if You're on Wordpress

These two Wordpress plugins are a great place to start:

    a. **WordPress SEO Plugin by Yoast:** This plugin is awesome, because it helps you rate your page SEO as you optimize your page. It will give you tips on how to optimize the post or page and, as you make the fixes, the rating will go from red (bad, like a pimple or the deficit in your bank account) to green (good, like the almighty avocado or the color of money). It also helps you improve "readability" by offering tips for simplifying sentences and creating better hierarchy. (www.Yoast.com/wordpress/seo/)

    b. **All in One SEO Pack by Michael Torbert:** This plugin has less features than the Yoast plugin but is still very effective for defining SEO titles, descriptions and keywords. (www.Wordpress.org/plugins/all-in-one-seo-pack/)

To correctly keyword your website pages, posts and portfolio entries, you'll need to do some research to find out the optimal keywords that people are searching to find a business site like yours. If you can figure out what phrases and keywords people are using to find content like yours, then you can start writing with those keywords in mind. Besides that, you can then type those keywords into the SEO plugin area on applicable posts and pages within your site so that search engines can more easily make the connection. If you are willing to learn about SEO, take some time to delve into Google AdWords' Keyword Planner. This tool lets you see what keywords and phrases people locally and universally are searching to get to sites in your industry and regarding your topic. It's a tool associated with Google Adwords, but you don't have to buy ads to use it. If used correctly, you can find the keywords you should target for your business. If you can't figure it out by yourself, hire (or set up a barter / trade with) an SEO consultant to help you research keywords you should be targeting for your site.

The most important thing when creating content, is that it's helpful, interesting, adds value to your target audience, and reflects well on you as a service provider. Don't just half-ass a blog because people say you should be blogging. Doing something just for the sake of it misses the mark. Document creative tips and shortcuts you use. If there's a topic or technique you keep getting asked about, write a tutorial. Give a behind-the-scenes look at your studio. When you share portfolio work, explain your process and procedures.

Between creating useful content and posting well-executed portfolio work regularly, you will start to encourage backlinks to your site. This will all snowball (albeit slowly, perhaps) into better visibility online.

Social Media: Your Ticket to Ride

Facebook, Twitter, Instagram, Pinterest, Dribbble, Behance, Medium—as a creative, all of these social media platforms are great tools to share your work, vision, and brand. They're especially magical places because they create opportunity for you to connect with peers, mentors, and potential clients from all over the world. You're not constrained to your regional acquaintances and cousins. You're goin' global, baby. Or at least there's the potential to. Each site allows you to link to your website, driving traffic to your portfolio and contact page. It's one of the easiest ways to organically build an audience and lure it to your online lair.

You probably already have personal accounts on most of these platforms. If you do, you might be wondering if you should just use the accounts you already have to promote your freelance work. It's up to you, really.

Whichever route you choose, use social media profiles to their full advantage! Starting a new account for your business from scratch is brutal, but doing it when your company is young is the best time to start. Lock down the handles, then start building the audience by letting your personal account followers know you've created the business profile. Curate your account to reflect the brand story you want to tell for you and your company. Then use your personal account to continue to remind friends who don't follow your company profile that you're doing great things over there.

GETTING A SEPARATE ACCOUNT FOR YOUR COMPANY

Pros:
- More privacy on your personal profiles
- You can build an audience that's unique to your creative work
- You can curate your brand story without personal life distractions

Cons:
- Double the work of posting and responding to comments
- Gaining a new following can be rough at first

PERSONAL PROFILES THAT DOUBLE AS WORK PROFILES

Pros:
- You already have a following built up
- Some of your existing audience, who wouldn't normally have followed a new work account, might be won over by seeing your work on your existing account
- If you're freelancing and doing business as your personal name, then using your personal account makes sense

Cons:
- More censure on what you post. What you may be cool with your friends seeing, you mayyyy not be cool with your client seeing.

Lock Down Your Username/Handles

When choosing your username on the various platforms, try as hard as you can to get the same username across the board. It makes it much easier when you promote your social media presence. But it's not a life or death thing if you can't make it happen. To search username availability, there are all kinds of handy online tools. One that we have used before is: www.Namecheckr.com.

Do the Social Media Cleanse

We've all Google stalked someone before. Don't act above it. You know how easy it is. You meet someone, you get curious, you awake from a trance two hours later with 45 internet tabs open containing various search results for your person of interest. Then there's that awkward moment when you accidentally mention something that they never disclosed to you, but you read in one of their Facebook posts from 2004. Our world has access to more and more personal information, thanks (or curses) to social media. Consider whether or not you want to make your personal accounts private, so that only close friends and family can see them. If not, then you'll need to review all your accounts and sweep them for incriminating evidence (i.e. anything a potential client could wince, flinch, grimace or SMH at).

According to the Career Builder study in 2017 by Harris Interactive, 70% of companies research potential hires on social networking sites. Why would their habit be much different when it comes to a freelancer like yourself? When they look you up, they are doing their due diligence to see if you are a fit for their needs. If they find something they don't like, the project you could have had is dust in the wind. Apparently, this happens a lot. According to the same study, 54% of hiring managers who currently research candidates via social media said they have found information that has caused them not to hire a candidate. If you are going to keep any of your accounts public as you start your new business, be aware of this, and follow our steps below to ready your profiles for outside scrutiny. We're not suggesting you be someone you're not just to get a job. We're just saying, maybe don't post that Boomerang of you lighting your fart on fire.

1. **Google yourself.** You might be surprised what accounts are still active that you don't even use anymore. Delete dormant accounts that you no longer update.

2. **On all social media profiles you keep, update the bio.** Mention your business. It doesn't have to be a hard sell to be professional. The ideal bio includes your business name, your title or creative specialty, and something fun or memorable about you. The tone of voice should match your brand identity positioning. Don't forget to link your dang website at the end!

3. **On your various profiles, remove anything that no longer reflects your talent level** (specifically talking about Behance and Dribbble here). If it's in a different style than you do now, but is still well done, keep it. You're mainly looking to purge any work that looks unskilled or amateur (obvious college projects included).

4. **Remove inappropriate statuses, tweets, photos, etc. that may turn off potential clients.** You might not think you have ever said anything that could ever be offensive to anyone, but we were all young and dumb once. What is inappropriate? Well, it depends on the person judging, but here's a good place to start:

    - Provocative photos
    - Photos or posts about drugs or overuse of alcohol
    - Harsh cursing or angry rants
    - Bad-mouthing of employers, employees, or clients
    - Discriminatory comments about race, gender, religion, sexual orientation, etc..
    - Proof of lies on resume (if you've said one thing on your website and then your social media says another, that's not going to do your reputation any favors).

Tailor Content Per Social Network

Different social media platforms have different benefits and angles. Here's a cheat sheet of the top social networks for creatives and what content works best per venue:

1. Twitter: A network for voicing opinions about your industry, your life, the world, your favorite GIFs, and trending pop culture news. This space can be great for connecting with pillars in your creative world. Most creatives are managing their own Twitter account, which means no gate keepers (aka secretaries, managers, PR agents, etc.). It's a much easier platform to connect with your heroes on because the amount of content creators is quite low in comparison to the number of overall users.

Many Twitter users are passive (ie: just scrolling through other people's posts, liking and retweeting) so it's much easier to stand out if you're an active participant (ie: commenting and creating your own tweets). On Instagram, well-known creatives get thousands of likes and comments per post. It's unlikely you'll get a personalized response from your creative hero there. But on Twitter, that same creative might only get 140 likes and even less comments on a tweet they write. Cutting through the noise is so much easier. If you have a unique voice and respond to their tweets in a clever way, they'll likely respond to you, or at least see your tweet. It's a magical place in that sense. Use Twitter to show you have well-formed opinions and thoughts on creativity, and the world around you. Also use it to give a glance into yourself as a human. Be playful and fun. Everything doesn't have to be work related. The best Twitter accounts are smart, silly, vulnerable, genuine, off-topic and work-related all at once.

2. Facebook: While personal Facebook profiles are mainly for family/friend interactions, a business page is where you can keep people apprised of projects you're working on, announce new products, and share behind the scenes process. Facebook gives you more space to explain and promote your work, unlike Twitter, which is bound to limited characters.

3. Instagram: This is perhaps the easiest of the networks for visual creatives. You can post progress shots, finished projects, pics of your team, before and after photo edits, excerpts of something you're writing, etc.. If you use the right hashtags on your content, you become more easily discoverable to new followers. Once you hit a certain number of followers, the numbers almost seem to perpetuate themselves. It's that herd mentality. Instagram Stories allow you to be more spontaneous and silly without worrying about the video living on your feed forever. This is the most unguarded way to connect with your audience and make a human connection, and thus it can be the most compelling. Instagram Live can be a great way to do quick tutorials or AMA-style interviews with your followers.

4. LinkedIn: While LinkedIn is the butt of so many networking jokes, it's also a tool still used by certain groups to fact check your resume and qualifications. It really does serve that purpose well if kept updated and current. As removed as it feels compared to the personal interactions of Twitter and Instagram, it's still good for keeping up with professional acquaintances. Building that network might serve you well down the road when you're looking for a connection or introduction to a certain person. Also, the platform makes asking for recommendations from connections and clients easy. A recommendation is basically a testimonial about you from someone who confirms they have worked with or for you. Getting these will validate your work ethic, and you can repurpose the blurbs in the testimonial section of your website. John Luu, the AIGA Houston Communications Director, makes a case for LinkedIn this way: *"If you have a fairly unique name and a LinkedIn profile, chances are your LinkedIn profile shows up in the number one spot when someone searches for you on Google. This is a pretty powerful personal brand management tool when you think about it."*

5. Pinterest: If you post your own work with proper attribution (your name and website), then this can be a very powerful tool to amplify the visibility of your work, your name, and the traffic to your site. 80% of pins on Pinterest are re-pins (according to a 2012 study by RJMetrics), so pin it first and pin it right. Pinterest also serves as a great tool for creating mood boards for clients when starting new projects.

6. Dribbble: This is an invite-only site for creatives to share works in progress and screenshots of their latest work. No one gets in without another creative drafting them and, in a way, guaranteeing their quality. It's a chance to gain street cred from your creative peers. The site was designed as a way to show progress shots of projects in the works. It has since become more of a site where creatives post finished projects. It's a great place for feedback if you are following/followed by the right people. Sure, there are a lot of blanket *"Rad!"* and *"Looks Awesome"* comments, but you can also get solid critique if you straight up ask for it in your post.

Share the kind of work you want to start getting hired for, because a lot of agencies search here for subcontractors. It's your chance to show off the chops you've been building but maybe haven't been hired for yet, without having to write a whole case study about it for your website. Seek a Dribbble invite from a friend who has one to spare or search Twitter for people who are giving away invites through creative competitions. Once you're on it, bring your A-game. Some of the best creatives of our generation are on there. Hoodzpah has gotten and continues to get a ton of quality work through the platform. You can pay extra to get a pro account that gives you added analytics on your profile, a "hire me" button on your profile, opportunity to sell products through the platform, as well as other perks. According to Dribbble's in-house analytics, in 2015 79.3% of designers for hire (with pro accounts) received work inquiries. Those are great odds. There's also a job board on the platform where companies can look for creative talent.

7. Medium: This is a blogging platform where creatives can write think pieces on their industry, go in depth on the process behind a certain project, analyze the success of a recent project, or discuss current events. If you're looking to establish yourself as a leader in your industry, here's a great place to clarify your unique positions and ideas.

8. Behance: Similar to Dribbble, Behance is a community where you can post your creative work. Behance is for more complete posts and case studies showing the various details and broad scope of your projects, as opposed to the small snapshots Dribbble was designed for. Companies like Google, Facebook, and MTV cruise Behance to find talent for their projects.

Take the time to design these posts out well. The way you post on Behance will likely mirror closely the posts you do on your own portfolio site as far as scale and depth of messaging. But Behance will most likely give you a much bigger audience than the organic traffic you get to your website. It will get so many more eyes on your work and the backlinks to your site will then boost your SEO.

These general guidelines are just the beginning. It'll take some trial and error to figure out what works for you, and what kind of unique content your audience wants, but with some helpful feedback from your followers, you'll soon figure out the perfect equation.

Tips for Using Social Media to Your Best Advantage:

1. Be genuine. Create work and posts that are authentic to you. You're more likely to get clients you'll vibe with if you're honest about your style and personal brand culture. Also, don't copy other people's work. You will be found out and then inevitably called out. The creative community is tight knit, vigilant and ready to go to arms for their fellow craftsman if they feel a wrong has been done. Know the difference between inspiration and copying.

2. Don't overshare. Feed clogging with mundane posts only distracts from your quality posts. Respect your audience's time and interest-level. One post a day is a good habit on Facebook and Instagram. Twitter can support more frequent posting providing it's quality content your audience is interested in. An Instagram story made up of 50 videos might be overkill.

3. Provide engaging, useful and interesting content. Remember, when it comes down to it, social media was meant to be fun. If users see you're constantly hard selling, they will stop listening or even stop following. Be focused and even-handed, mixing business with fun, interesting info that adds value to your audience. Invest in them, not just yourself.

4. Post about self-initiated projects to fill in the gaps of your portfolio. Want to get logo work? Do a personal project and create a logo for it. Then share it across social media. Often, you get inquiries on what you put out there. If you don't have the portfolio work that shows you can do something, create a self-initiated project to prove you can.

5. Be an ally for your friends and they'll return the favor. This is not a tit for tat kind of equation. It's more of an implied system. If your friend just opened the brewery they've been building for the past year and you share a post about it to all your followers, it's very likely that when you launch a new endeavor they will feel moved to support you in kind. You have talented and connected friends doing very cool things (hopefully?) and they're your allies as much as your avenue to potential clients. Support them and they will support you. Maybe not all the time, but sometimes. The by-product of this is brand alignment. The people you support and align yourself with become a means that others can use to character reference you and your business.

6. Use hashtags. And use them correctly! It helps people discover your work on these platforms and will grow your audience beyond the people already following you. Don't go crazy, just use a handful that best apply to the content piece. Try and come up with a catchy, short, easy-to-remember hashtag for your own company. We use #Hoodzpah on every piece of content we post. And we created the hashtag #FABAS for this very book (soft sell to tag us, yo).

7. Embrace the two-way conversation. If someone responds to your post, write them back. Even if it's just an emoji of recognition. Followers love to know they've been heard and appreciated by you. Also, comment on other people's posts. Engage with peers and brands you want to work with. Staying on their radar in a supportive way will come back in spades.

8. Social media is a place for like-minded people, not just friends. Follow people you admire or want to work with. Start interfacing with them. That being said, be unique! Don't just say *"love your work!"* That puts you immediately in the fan position. And what can they say back to that? *"Thanks"* is about it for that conversation killer. Rather, add something to the conversation. Show you understand and appreciate their process as a peer while still telling them how great their work is. Give them a seed to keep the convo going.

9. Beware of the Tumblr feed creep. Tumblr belongs on Tumblr. Don't turn YOUR social media presence into a tumblr of other people's work. Half the time people don't read captions and may not realize you're not posting your own work. Post your work and be authentically you. If you do post something by someone else you better credit it and tag it and be sure you have permission from the creator.

10. Consider your tone. You're allowed to have opinions. You're human and there are many important conversations that can happen online. Just remember that without the context of your in-person face and mannerisms, things can easily be misunderstood. What you think is a harmless joke or sarcastic remark could be taken as a blatant insult by someone else. Social media can turn into the Thunderdome in milliseconds. Proceed with caution and consider the result of careless remarks.

11. Death to bots! Tailor your posts for each social media venue. Also, resist the urge to use bots that like and auto-comment for you. People WILL notice when your bot writes *"great shot!"* on their sentimental post about the passing of their Meemaw. Make the time to do it yourself or hire a social media manager to help you. Just say *"no"* to bots.

Content Strategy

Plan out your content calendar. If your strategy is a mix of social media, blogging, and portfolio posts, put together a calendar listing when you'll post what. Then create draft posts with your content and images ready to roll. Social media can be fun to do off the cuff at times, but having the majority of your content prepared ahead of time helps you stay active online even when your work week gets swamped. Choose a slow time in your month to plan this out. There are great apps out there that can help you plan social (We use Later app).

As a small business owner you're busy. If you're overwhelmed with the amount of social media networks to tackle, choose your top three you want to invest time in to start to maximize your time and efforts. We recommend at least one of the portfolio sites (Behance or Dribbble) and then two of the others. If those gain good results after a few months, it will help motivate you to look into the other platforms.

Research brands you look up to. Research companies similar to yours. What do you like and dislike about how they run their social. Create a Likes and Dislikes list, gathering your thoughts on what you want to try and what you want to avoid based on your research. Keep your list as a cheat sheet to help guide you in your content strategy. When you come across posts that impress you, continue to update your list to better understand the methods behind what makes for good social media communication.

Measuring Your Social Media Success

Analyze the in-platform analytics to see how you're doing in your social media strategy and to figure out what content your viewers are connecting with best. Pivot your approach based on what works. Besides these data sources, install Google Analytics (www.Google.com/analytics) on your website to see your referral traffic from social media all in one place. With Google Analytics you can see all your traffic sources and learn about your audience, their habits, and behavior on your site. There are whole books and blogs dedicated to Google Analytics. Learn the basics of how to read the data, then use it to your advantage in content planning.

When Social Media Stabs You in the Back

The internet can be a wily place. One way or another, your work is likely to get dispersed. Should your work get shared or used on social without credit/permission, don't lose your cool...yet. First, try dealing with the party sharing/using your work without your permission in private via DM or email. Be calm and concise in your initial email. More often than not, they will reply with the intent to make things right. It seems unthinkable, but it happens all the time and sometimes the offenders are unaware that their work is a rip off. We've had to deal with numerous cases like this. One person told us, *"I only used your work as inspiration."* She had live-traced a logo we designed and placed her own client name into it and she was genuinely shocked that this was copyright infringement. There's a lot of misinformed, uneducated creatives out there.

If they ignore your message or respond wrongly, then it's time to let them know that you are prepared to take legal action. Download a boiler plate Cease and Desist document. Customize the key points as they relate to your circumstance, and then send that to the person. If they still do not respond, reach out to your legal advisor for next steps.

A thought on social media as a forum for public shaming: More and more we're seeing people bypassing legal methods for trial by social media, mainly in response to plagiarism or misuse of uncredited work. Calling out a creative thief publicly on social media can result in enough pressure and bad press from your network of friends and peers (and their friends and peers) to force the offender to take the ripped work down. Just be careful and think hard before using this tactic. It's great for pressuring Goliath companies that have more money and legal power than you do, the way Tuesday Bassen did with Zara. If, however, the public shaming is pointed at a young and unenlightened creative student who ripped one of your designs, this could ruin them and have permanent lasting consequences that you can't foresee. Once it's on the internet it's nearly impossible to undo. Yes, it was 100% wrong of them to steal/use your work without your consent. But public shaming has very real and very lasting consequences and can easily turn into cruel and unusual punishment. So just consider all possible scenarios and try all other avenues before you resort to this, if at all.

Chapter Checklist: To Do

- [ ] Decide between new social profiles, or using your existing personal profiles. Choose your handles/usernames if getting new accounts.

- [ ] Do the social media cleanse.

- [ ] Choose which social networks best fit you and your business (tackle 2 or 3 to start).

- [ ] Plan out your content calendar. Research brands you admire to get cues on how they're using social media effectively. Adapt your findings to your own brand identity and story.

- [ ] Do a little research on keywords and test out the Google AdWords' Keyword Planner. Install an SEO plugin on your site, if your site supports one.

- [ ] Post on social media that you are taking on new clients.

- [ ] Reach out to five friends/acquaintances personally who you think might benefit from your services. A text, an email, a DM, whatever is appropriate for your relationship. Keep it light and friendly. *"Hey Kelly, I saw you're opening a new shop. Congrats! If you're looking for design help, let me know. Maybe we can figure out a trade."*

- [ ] Reach out to five dream clients via a contact form or cold email. Then follow people who work at that company on social to stay in touch. Try and comment/tweet to these people regularly to build familiarity.

Blank page,

Blank page,

A sheet like bone.

Blank page,

Blank page,

Like Macaulay, alone*.

*A reference to Home Alone, *not to Macaulay himself, who we hope never feels alone.*

Contract
I.
III.
VI.
XI.
A.
B.
C.
VII
Signed In Blood Forever...
It's Fine...really.
X

9
Contracts

*Part rules of engagement,
part prenup.*

———

Disclaimer: We are not lawyers. Nor have we played any on TV. So, just know that the information we're about to share with you is not legal advice. It's only research we've done on these topics for our own business. These are our thoughts on the subject from our own experience and hard knock lessons. But consult with your legal advisor to decide what is right for you personally, especially concerning how you write and execute your contracts.

Always, always, always sign a contract before starting a project. Even an as-played-on-TV lawyer would agree with that. You should never start a job without some formal signed agreement showing mutual understanding between creative and client about the rules of engagement. If a potential client is trying to avoid signing a contract, this is a giant red flag. For centuries, cultures have been using agreements and contracts to conduct business. This is not a novel thing. It's a part of commerce and we do it every day. When you sign a credit card receipt, you're signing a contract. When you click "I agree" as you install your latest iOS update, you're signing a contract. In order to get a driver's license, rent an apartment, buy a home, or open a bank account, you have to sign a contract. A good contract protects both the creative and the client. It shouldn't be scary, but rather reassuring for both parties. It means both sides will get what they want, providing they do what they agreed to do. Anyone trying to avoid this is either a little naive or at least a little nefarious.

Get contract templates for your most commonly performed services. Then customize them for each unique client. This will save you oodles of time. Like, enough time to have a *The Simpsons* marathon with a *Law & Order* marathon chaser. After you quote a project and the client says "yes," you don't want their ardour to get cold while you try and create your Magna Carta from scratch. Would you propose to your dreamboat on the jumbotron at Yankee stadium, receive the good news, and then leave everyone in suspense to go forge an engagement ring? Nay. You've got to have the ring ready, and you get it fitted once they say yes.

Contract Resources

You can get surprisingly far creating your own contract drafts by looking at examples online. Definitely talk to your lawyer for final tweaks and revisions. Here are some resources to help you get started:

Smashing Magazine's *The Collective Legal Guide for Designers (Contract Samples)* shows specific examples of contracts for all kinds of design work. The examples are free, and link to editable documents so you can customize and download them for your own use. Google the title to find it online.

AIGA, the professional association for design, also created a set of master agreements, along with variations customized for the most popular design projects and services in our industry. Their contracts contain intense legalese and are quite thorough.

Key Things Contracts Should Include

The following are some of the most important elements you'll want to be sure are included in your contract based on our business experience:

1. Your legal business name, and the client's legal business name: Get it right because you can't enforce a contract against someone who doesn't legally exist.

2. Price, expenses, payment terms, and payment schedule: How much will you be paid and when (at specific milestones, or on certain dates)? Are you charging the client for expenses that are not included in the project cost? Outline what the expenses could be and specify if there is an expense spending cap. If the client is late in paying your invoices, what are the fees or consequences? Tip: large companies like Target or Disney usually have very strict net 30-60 payment terms (meaning they have up to 30 or 60 days to pay your invoice once the project is finished). If it's not a reputable company you are familiar with, get an initial payment up front. We require partial payment up front for 90% of the jobs we do. The other 10% are bigger dream clients who just won't accept those terms. With small to mid-sized companies, getting an initial payment up front is a show of good faith that is very standard. It's a good way to ensure the client has the money they say they do to cover the project you're working on.

3. Schedule: If you and your client have agreed to meet a specific delivery date, or make certain milestone goals, then include those in the agreement. To keep yourself protected from delays caused by the client, include copy reminding them that deadlines are a two-way street. If they don't meet their deadlines or supply the necessary feedback/info/copy in a timely manner, then you shouldn't be required to still meet your deadline with only a fraction of the time you had anticipated. Timeliness is a responsibility for both parties.

4. The scope of work and final deliverables: What work, specifically, does the agreement cover and what final files/assets/native (workable editable) files will you deliver to the client? Be thorough about how many concepts, rounds of revisions, meetings, final designs, file types, etc.. the project will include. If you don't create black and white boundaries, the limits of what you're expected to do are left up to speculation. You can even include a list of what is "not included" in the scope, and list add-on fees or services the client can request which fall outside the scope.

5. Kill fees and termination clause: If one of the parties wants to end the contract before the project is completed, what are the terms and conditions? What do they owe you if they end the project early? Do you get to keep the initial upfront payment? We outline kill fees based on how much of the project is completed. "If terminated after round 1, $xxx is still owed..., if terminated after round 2 $xxxx is still owed" and so on. Also make sure you explain if or how copyright will be handled on partially completed work if the project is terminated. Do they get working files? Do they get nothing? Up to you. Just be clear. You might also consider an option for you to terminate the project if the client is non-responsive for 30 days. It happens more often than you'd think, and can negatively affect your scheduling and workflow.

6. Specify the state that will govern the contract: This is more important if you and your client are in different states or different countries. Different states have different laws, and having your home state oversee any litigation about your contract is desirable as far as convenience and familiarity of laws. For international contracts, definitely have a lawyer advise you on special precautions to take.

7. A "force majeure" clause: This will protect you from unforeseen catastrophic events and "Acts of God" that inhibit you from performing your work as promised, to no fault of your own. For example, if your home gets caught in the path of a tornado and your computer and backup drives are destroyed, you don't want to be held liable for missing an agreed upon deadline.

8. An "indemnity" clause: If damages result from something the client does related to the agreement, you want the client to hold you/your company harmless from claims, costs, and expenses associated with it. For example, if the client uses your work beyond the allowed licensing terms in the contract, you don't want to be responsible for attorney's fees you'll have to pay to take them to court about it.

You also want to be careful about wording any indemnity clause holding your client harmless for work you make that infringes on someone else's rights. Many lawsuits have happened because of unintentional similarities of work despite a creative's best efforts to make something unique. If you do include a clause like this for your client, limit it to something saying you will create work that doesn't infringe "to the best of the artist's knowledge and belief," as worded and suggested by the Graphic Artists Guild contract glossary. This protects you in case you had no knowledge of a similar work to one you create for a client.

9. A severability clause: If one part of your contract is deemed unenforceable or void by a court, this clause ensures that the rest of the contract remains in effect. One misstep shouldn't nullify the rest. You wouldn't throw a whole avocado away because of one tiny bruise—you'd cut out the bad part and make some tasty guacamole with the rest!

10. Copyright and licensing terms: In the U.S., you are automatically considered the author and owner of anything you make as a freelancer, unless you state in the contract otherwise. In the copyright and licensing section of your contract you'll want to outline the following:

    a. **Rights:** What rights to the final artwork are you transferring to the client? Partial or full rights?

    b. **Media limitations:** Sometimes you'll want to limit the usage rights to a certain kind of media, i.e. print and online, only print, only on the client's website, only on soft goods/apparel, only on hats, etc..

    c. **Exclusivity limitations:** If you're licensing a work to someone, be clear about whether they have the sole right to license that work for a time or in a certain area or on a certain medium, etc.. If they want exclusivity like that, it usually costs more for them to get it, because it means you can't license the work to anyone else within those parameters.

d. **Numbers limitations:** You can limit how many times your work is printed, seen, or used within those media rights. For example, the client can use your illustration on t-shirts only, and can only print and sell up to 50,000 units. After that, they have to seek a new licensing agreement with you for further use.

e. **Location limitations:** You may want to restrict a client's rights to use your work only in a specific country or region. Why? Well if a regional Italian t-shirt company wants to license your design for their fall line, you might not want this to limit your ability to also sell the design to a company in the USA.

f. **Time limitations:** Can they only "license" the work to use for a window of time? For example, perhaps you license a photo to a greeting card company to use on holiday cards during only the months of September through December of a certain year. On the other hand, you could transfer rights "in perpetuity" to a client, so they can use it forever. The latter is a good clause for logo designs, being as the client should own their logo and be free to use it to any extent without added fees, forever.

g. **Ownership of original art:** There is a difference between reproduction rights and the original work. If you've made an original illustration using charcoal, you may want to retain rights to sell the original artwork while also licensing the digital version of the art to clients to reproduce.

h. **When do the agreed rights transfer?** At Hoodzpah, we stipulate that rights agreed to in the contract only go into effect once full payment for those rights are received. This way, if the client doesn't pay their invoice, we have leverage.

11. Reservation of rights: This clause goes below your copyright and licensing terms, and states that any rights not explicitly granted, remain with you the creator. This is assumed by the law, but it's good to state it emphatically. For example, you might state here that unchosen concepts or photos or initial sketches remain in your ownership and are not included with the one final artwork rights outlined in previous sections.

12. Moral rights: According to the Graphic Artists Guild contract glossary (available on their website under "Tools + Resources"), the four rights covered by this clause are "1) the right to protect the work from modifications that would harm the reputation of the artist; 2) the right of attribution, so that authorship is acknowledged; 3) the right of disclosure, to control presentation of artwork to the public; 4) the right of recall, to withdraw or disavow a work if it is changed." This section also covers your right to show the work you create for the client in your portfolio. This is a huge right to retain as a professional. If a client should pay more if they want to negotiate away your rights to attribution and to display your work in your portfolio. It's not in your best interest, as displaying the work could generate more work for you.

13. Declare it the full agreement: Make sure you put a period on the contract by declaring that it is the complete agreement. Also include how changes to the agreement can be made.

Consider E-Sign Technology

Who wants to print out a contract, sign it, scan it in, gather the scans into a PDF, send it to the client, and then have them do the same rigmarole on their end? If you have an Adobe Creative Cloud subscription, then you have the most recent version of Adobe Acrobat, which includes e-sign technology within it. Just open any PDF and click on the "fill & sign" tab to open the e-sign options. Then you can send the e-signed doc to the other party for their signatures, and download the final record once it's finished. Making these annoying tasks easy for clients makes it much more likely you'll get timely signatures so you can get rolling on your project and make that cheddar.

Worried about the validity of e-sign technology? According to the E-SIGN act of 2000, *"a signature, contract, or other record relating to such transaction may not be denied legal effect, validity, or enforceability solely because it is in electronic form; and (2) a contract relating to such transaction may not be denied legal effect, validity, or enforceability solely because an electronic signature or electronic record was used in its formation."* Adobe explains the legality of e-signatures compared to wet signatures on its blog in an article called "'This is legal, right?' - Electronic Signatures & The Law." It concludes, *"an electronic signature and a wet ink signature are equivalent in most respects, and they can be brought into trial."* Still, it continues with the warning that all signatures will be scrutinized for their admissibility, whether wet or digital. *"Does it represent the intent of the signatory? Has the document been altered? Who had the right to sign this document? How was the signature derived, and what controlled access to the document for its signature? These questions come into play no matter the type of signature."* If you do go with e-signing, cut down on your risk by using a credible software to perform the e-sign (like Adobe), and ensure that the person signing has the authority to sign on behalf of their company.

Chapter Checklist: To Do

- ☐ Look up the contract resources mentioned above, and download the three contract templates that apply most to your services.
- ☐ Contact a lawyer to get help customizing the contracts to suit your needs.
- ☐ Test the e-sign technology of Adobe Acrobat or a similar solution.
- ☐ Figure out what licensing terms you feel comfortable with for your 3 most common service types.

GET IT TOGETHER

10
Workflow Mojo

Taking a project from contract to completion.

———

Being "right-brained" or "creative" should never be used as a crutch. It's not a sick note to get out of gym. Don't segregate your capable imagination from organized method. They're not in rival gangs. In fact, they're star-crossed lovers. They long for each other, and write poems and acoustic love songs for one another. Creativity thrives within consistency and structure. Creative Mad Genius + Method = Enviable Entrepreneur.

Creatives are the perfect entrepreneurial candidates. Think about it: most entrepreneurs spend a ton of cash on identity design, creating a website, making sales collateral, building a social media presence, and crafting a unique brand experience. These are things many creatives can do innately and we don't charge ourselves a penny when we perform these services for ourselves. As creatives, we relish solving problems in a way that delights the intended audience. This is the core of what great entrepreneurship is all about. Embrace the fact that you are the best candidate to run your own show and be your own boss. You have all the qualifications you never knew you needed. Once you get your everyday systems and procedures in order, you'll be a force of nature to be reckoned with.

Setup a Quote to Completion Workflow for Jobs

As a creative, you are the navigator, captain, and mechanic of your client's journey. Every job you work on will have a unique set of parameters and basic milestones. Even though the type of work might change, you'll always find a steady, loyal friend in a well-organized workflow.

A Typical Workflow at Hoodzpah

1. **Potential client requests a quote.**

2. **We respond to the potential client in a timely manner and gather more information to quote them.** We aim for 24 hour response times for emails, even if it means just responding to say "thanks for writing in and we'll be back in touch soon with questions and more info." That buys you a day or two to get caught up and get back to them with the real questions. This includes asking about the goals of the project, the scope, the timeline, and the budget.

3. **Once all info is in hand, send quote/proposal to client.** Familiarize yourself with how the person or company perceives value so you can best present your proposal in terms that appeal to them. As we mentioned before, contextualizing the price helps the client justify the cost. This is why it's important to learn about the business and the goal of the project before you quote them. It helps you make a compelling case. For more on this, refer back to *Chapter 4: Pricing and Proposals* chapter.

4. **Did client agree to your proposal? Yay! Proceed on to step 5.** Did client decline due to budget? Suggest a lower rate for a simplified scope if you still want the job. Did the client reject the proposal indefinitely? Don't stress out. Quoting is not an exact science. The perfect proposal could be rejected by a client on any whim, and a mediocre proposal could win over another client on an equal but opposite whim. Even if a client doesn't choose you, wish them the best and stay on their radar in a positive way. You'd be surprised how many people decline our quote, thinking we're overpriced or under-experienced, only to return in a year after a bad experience with someone who was cheaper or more seemingly-qualified.

5. **Sign a contract with the client.** You get to use that contract you just spent hours editing and building. Once signed, save the contract in a safe place within your client folder so you can easily refer back to it later. If the client tries to expand the scope, you'll have it quickly on hand to remind them of what you agreed to. Also if you end up in a legal suit with the client, you'll want to know exactly where your contract is. Do not proceed on any work until you have the contract in hand!

6. **Send your w-9 to the new client for their tax records.** A w-9 is an IRS form that lets the client know how to report their work with you to the government. It shows your business structure, your legal business name, tax identification number and address. Have one of these ready to give to every company you work with. If you do over $600 of work with them, they'll need it so they can send you a 1099 at the end of the year, which will recap all your transactions together. Sending this at the beginning of the job saves your client the hassle of having to chase you down for it come tax season. Make your client's life as easy as possible.

7. **If the work you're doing will be paid on a project-based / flat rate, send an invoice for the down payment on the job before starting any work.** In your contract, you should have outlined your payment plan, and specified what kind of down payment you expect. For most jobs, we require half up front. For higher price tag jobs, a unique payment plan can be negotiated that works for both parties. Just make sure you're on the same page. As we previously mentioned, larger companies will likely be strict on a net 30 or net 60 payment schedule, without any down payment. You probably can't expect a down payment with those types of companies. At that point, you can either trust the reputation of their name and do the work in anticipation of payment at the end, or you can pass up the opportunity if you don't feel comfortable or you don't have the cash-flow to wait for payment.

8. **Do your research, confirming your goals with the client.** We call it the discovery phase. Before starting any creative work, do a deep dive on your client to learn key things about the client's company and project. This is a much more in-depth version of the preliminary research you did to quote them:

- Competitors
- Target audience
- Values
- Core problem to be solved through the project (main goal)
- Criteria for success
- Criteria for failure

Review your research with the client and have them sign off on your findings. It's important to be in agreement on the main goal of the project. Why? Because it makes getting feedback and approvals much easier. When you've agreed on a main goal, then all proofs can be critiqued based on how the work supports or detracts from achieving that main goal. This simple test helps to quickly separate valid feedback from subjective opinions. It also helps to define a clear end zone, so you can easily prove when your work is a success.

9. **Create and present your work.** It's finally time to make something! Proceed through scope of work. As you send the client proofs, remind them which stage or phase of the project you're on, so they're always in remembrance of the agreed upon parameters. Don't just send a proof without context. Let them know what feedback you want from them, so you don't get feedback you don't need (or that distracts from the main goal). In the proof presentation, show how the work meets the main goal initially agreed upon in the discovery phase. Frame the work in terms of the parameters you outlined together for a successful outcome. And remember: as much as possible, present proofs in person or verbally over the phone. Your client is busy and most likely won't read the notes on each page of the proof, or even the email it was attached to. It's the age of skimming so being able to explain the proofs in person or over the phone will help avoid any miscommunication, plus it will give you the chance to guide them in the best direction.

10. **Send invoices if you have milestone payments scheduled between your down payment and your final payment.** If the client becomes delinquent in their payments, stop all work and don't deliver any files until they catch up. Be strict about your payment rules to engender a respect for healthy boundaries. If delinquency persists, seek legal help.

11. **Once final approval is given on the project, or your scope limit is reached, send final invoice.**

12. **After final payment is made, send final deliverables to the client.** Gather the final files in a well-organized and labelled folder and send to the client in a format they can easily access (we prefer sharing via Dropbox). If scope limit is reached and the client requests further changes or creative work, agree to a new flat rate or ongoing hourly rate before continuing. You might choose to wait until initial scope invoices are paid before proceeding.

13. **At the end of the job, clean up the project folder and backup files. Our post job clean up looks like this:**

    1. Delete unnecessary assets (photos or files we didn't use at all).

    2. Archive unchosen options.

    3. Save crucial emails about changes and approvals to the folder.

    4. Keep the final files in a clearly marked main folder.

    5. Back up the files: if we know we won't work with the client any time soon, we will back up the files to an external hard drive to make room for new projects. Sometimes this is easier to do monthly rather than as each project finishes.

14. **Check in on the project after it launches.** You should be interested in knowing if the work was well received and got the results you anticipated. Don't be afraid to send an email to your client to see how things are going. They'll be glad to know you're invested in their success.

15. **Post a case study about the work on your portfolio and bask in your accomplishments.** Well-earned gloating is fairly self-explanatory, right?

Organizing Your Project Files

With every new project, you'll need to create a job folder on your computer where your project will live. If you do this haphazardly, you'll be facing a logistical nightmare before you can say, "Cheesecake Factory hangover." Can you imagine what it'd be like trying to drive through a country that didn't have regulated street signs and traffic codes? Yikes. Having a structured way of navigating your files is just as important. Save your sanity and figure out a system for file organization.

At Hoodzpah, This is How We Organize Our Files:

We have two main folders on our company drive.

1. **"Hoodzpah Internal"** - Where we store our own marketing assets, brand files, social media material, talks and workshop materials, this book, and the like.

2. **"Clients"** - Where we store our most recent project files for clients (old work is archived on backup drives). Within this main "Clients" folder, we have five sub folders that group clients alphabetically in chunks (A-D, E-K, L-P, Q-T, U-Z) so we can navigate faster than scrolling through a bulk list. Each client then has its own labelled folder.

Each project for the client has its own folder within the client folder. The individual job folder is broken into sub-folders like "Business" for contracts, email archives, and legal stuff, "Assets" or "Working" for inspiration, tools, and mock-ups used in the project; and then a folder for each round of the project as it progresses (Round 1, Round 2, etc.).

📁 Clients
📁 A-D
📁 Dr. Crane Psychology
📁 Business
📁 Logo
📁 Round 1
📁 Working
📁 E-K
📁 L-P

Organize your files based on what works best for you, but be sure the system is consistent and intuitive, so you can find things easily. Your files should be user-friendly so that if you grow your team everyone can easily jump into the system and find their way.

Tips for Organizing Project Files

1. **This might sound obvious, but be sure to name all files consistently and correctly so that it is easy to search for them later on.** A computer's search function is thorough, but not telepathic. The file name should contain the client name (or a common acronym for it), the project name (or a consolidated moniker for it), and the proof round or version number. i.e.: "Nicolettos_logo_v1.ai" for example.

2. **Never leave off till tomorrow what you can do today.** Don't lazily store a project asset on your desktop or in your default downloads folder, assuming you'll place it in the correct file later. You'll forget. You'll have the best intentions, but you'll forget. Avoid broken links and wild goose chases by placing it in the correct folder from the get go.

3. **When working on a file, keep versions of files, in case a client changes their mind and wants to return to an old proof.** We usually keep all versions until a job is final and paid for. Then we consolidate versions down to only the pertinent ones.

4. **Keep records of your client's feedback and approvals within the job folder. It bears repeating!** Save emails with important approvals and feedback to your project folder. This paper trail might save your butt if a client is looking for a scapegoat to blame for their frustrations. Having timestamped logs of their requests and approvals is also key in case you ever get into a legal battle over a project.

Time Management

Logging your time is an annoying task. However, it's necessary if you are charging by the hour (you have to know how much to invoice) and crucial to analyzing the accuracy of your flat rate quote once you've finished a job (to make sure you were profitable). That being said, don't forget to time track your non-billable hours too. You might be surprised at how much time you're spending outside of client work to run the business. Knowing where you're allocating time can help you decide when to hire, and help you better plan your work weeks. There are tons of free apps that can help you with time tracking. We use one called Trigger (www.TriggerApp.com) because it integrates into our accounting software, which means invoicing hourly rate clients is easy and painless.

Managing Responsibilities and Scheduling

Growing your business is exciting. More projects mean more money, right? It also means more expectations to meet. In the rush of new jobs, you might accidentally forget existing responsibilities on older projects. Keeping tabs on all your clients and projects is important. Here's how:

Create a project run-sheet. At Hoodzpah, we used to have a Google Spreadsheet that we updated weekly. Now we use a web app called Monday. They both served the same purpose: an instant snapshot of our business's jobs on deck. The run-sheet has fields for:

- Client
- Contact Name for Client
- Project Name
- Status of the Job (In progress, waiting on client, proof out, invoiced, etc.)
- Project's flat rate or hourly rate
- Payment Dates
- Assigned Creative(s)
- Total Hours budgeted for the project to make a profit (if it's flat rate)

If you want software with more bells and whistles for project management, there are many online apps that support project collaboration, to do lists, proof approvals, and scheduling. Just type in "project management software" into an online search. Trello, Basecamp, Asana, and Monday are just a few of the awesome options out there, each with different features.

Create a job calendar. Google Calendar is a great free way to organize goal deadlines and map out your jobs so that you stay on top of sending out proofs, checking on clients for feedback (you'll have to remind a lot of clients to get back to you), and delivering files. You can set text or email reminders for yourself so that you don't get behind on your jobs. You can add people to the calendar so your whole team gets updates. Also setup a calendar for internal jobs like a blogging schedule, a website update schedule, a schedule for reconciling the books, for preparing quarterly taxes, preparing 1099s, even a schedule for preparing gifts or cards for clients in time to send out for holidays, etc.. Some of the project management apps mention before include great scheduling tools as well.

Create personal "to do" lists. Your job run sheet and calendar are great for a high-level view of your business workload and timeline. Motivate yourself on a micro-level, too: keep your own daily to do list, give yourself manageable goals to meet and relish in your success as you check them off. There are so many great apps for this on desktop and mobile. You can keep an old school, hard copy agenda, too. Daily task management is massive in the overall battle of meeting deadlines on your larger job calendar.

Chapter Checklist: To Do

- ☐ Create your business folder, alphabetical client folders, etc.
- ☐ Create a project runsheet in Google Docs or your preferred job management software.
- ☐ Create your job calendar.
- ☐ Download the most recent W-9 form from the IRS and fill it out.

The ART of COMMUNICATION

Step 1: LISTEN FIRST.

Step 2: See Step 1.

11
Communication and Collaboration

Reaching across the aisle.

―

Avoiding Communication Breakdown

As a freelancer or business owner, you're the face of your company. You don't have an HR department to smooth over your indiscretions which means you have to be conscious of what you say, how you speak, and what you do. You'll deal with all kinds of people from all walks of life while doing business. Each one has a unique way they like to be talked to, and a unique idea of what is "appropriate" and "professional". Your goal is to meet them where they're at and make them feel comfortable while still being true to who you are. Mutual respect is key. Honest, fair dealings are a must. Remember, your brand hinges on the relationship your client has with you and your company. Communication missteps to watch out for:

Cussing

You can be professional without being a tool and you can be "real" without sounding like a Tarantino character. That's definitely not to say cursing isn't allowed, it's more just to say: proceed with caution and know your audience. After all, sometimes a well-placed curse really seals the deal. Other times it shows you the f*%$ing door.

Oversharing

Ooft. Clients don't need to know how poor you are or how horrible your last Tinder date went, just like they don't need to know that you woke up hungover in a gutter this morning. As our wise Grandmother says, "Show some pride. Don't air all your dirty laundry." It's healthy to keep some distance between you and your clients when it comes to personal details. The invisible wall of professionalism makes them think twice before texting you about revisions on a Saturday night, or expecting you to do them favors on pricing.

Gossiping and Whining

Don't speak negatively about clients (or anyone, really) in front of other clients. They'll assume you do the same about them to others. A gossipy conversation tells a client you don't respect people's privacy and reflects poorly on your trustworthiness. Telling people about fallouts with former bosses or business relationships is a big no-no. The right small talk and personal connection can go a long way, but don't treat work meetings like a mean girl sleepover.

Takeaway: Just keep things positive, find common ground that you both can relate on, and don't let conversation devolve into gossip, ranting, whining, fatalism, or too much Nietzsche.

"How do people, like, not curse? How is it possible? There are these gaps in speech where you just have to put a "fuck." I'll tell you who the most admirable people in the world are: newscasters. If that was me, I'd be like, "And the motherfuckers flew the fucking plane right into the Twin Towers." How could you not, if you're a human being? Maybe they're not so admirable. Maybe they're robot zombies."

- Nick Hornby, *A Long Way Down*

Email, Meeting or Phone Call?

Some people want to meet in person about everything, some avoid calls at all costs. You probably know what camp you fall in, but try to be flexible when it comes to communicating with clients. For people who prefer the phone, you'll likely get better feedback from them if you review proofs on the phone or over a video chat. After the call / video chat, write up a recap about what decisions you made and then email it to your client, asking them to simply confirm what you reviewed, so you have a paper trail to refer to later.

The more important moments of your client relationship are better handled through in-person meetings, video calls, or phone calls: presenting pivotal proofs, reviewing a project proposal, or talking about project problems, for example. In those moments, being able to see the client's face and talk to them audibly will help you make the most of intonation, tone, and non-verbal cues. Be very cautious of letting a client claim too much of your time, though. Phone calls, emails and meetings are a necessary part of any project. But every round of changes doesn't require an in-person meeting that lasts an hour. Breaking up your day to drive to their office or meet somewhere to review every single edit will really start detracting from your working hours and energy. Consider limiting how many in-person meetings you can accommodate in your project scope, and tie those meetings to important milestones (project kickoff, round 1 review, pre-press check, etc.). If a certain client wants to claim more of your time than the project scope allows, then they can pay you hourly for your extra time. Don't feel bad about this. As a service provider, your time is very precious. It directly correlates to how much income you can make, and it is limited.

Used properly, emails can be an invaluable tool. Used improperly, emails are like a Hydra. Write one bad one, and ten spawn in its place. Join us in making a stand for efficient, comprehensive emails! They should be short, sweet, and well organized. None of us have enough hours in the day, but we can claim some of them back if we can get this email beast under control.

Email Like a Champ

1. **Use subject lines correctly.** Include the project name at the very least, so it's easy to search for. Besides that, you might include the round name, or a small teaser of what you'll be talking about. "Project Name: Round 1 Proof." "Project Name: Assets Needed to Start."

2. **Be specific when you write.** Watch out for vague words like "this," "that," "he," "she," or "it." Sending a vague email means more back and forth questions and lost momentum.

3. **Make the email easy to skim with smart formatting.** Most people are busy and an email with more than one paragraph is scarier than being 59 minutes into your

1 hour complimentary airport Wi-Fi. They'll push it aside to be dealt with later, and intentionally or unintentionally move it to the bottom of their priorities.

- Use bulleted lists to keep things quick and to the point.
- Use short paragraphs so that information is broken up in nice digestible chunks according to topic.
- Bold or highlight your key, actionable requests.

4. **Include your email signature with contact information at the bottom of every email.** Make it easy for clients to contact you by phone or find your work online.

5. **Consider attachment file size.** If at all possible, don't send emails with attachments over 1MB. If you need to send larger files, consider using a file transfer service like www.Wetransfer.com, or link to the file on Dropbox.

6. **Be personable!** Remember what your client or collaborators are interested in and take a minute to connect to them human-to-human. It reminds them that we're all playing on the same team. Whether you connect over sports, *The Bachelor*, or cooking, add in a line or two of water-cooler talk at the beginning or end of your email.

7. **A note on email intros:** Before doing an email intro, check with each party individually to make sure the intro is okay. *Then* email and cc: everyone.

8. **Reread before hitting send.** Just once. One reread will save you a lot of heartache or embarrassment. You'll catch silly mistakes (that pesky "your" posing as "you're"), forgotten attachments, redundant sentences, or language that's too firm or too desperate. Taking that extra minute might save you four more emails to explain yourself afterwards.

Texting Clients: Proceed with Caution

Once opened, the texting floodgate is a tough one to close. In this day and age, texting is an inseparable part of communication. But when it comes to business, it's rarely necessary to use texts. This might be personal preference, but texting is the least ideal form of communication with your client. It can become invasive, since most people expect an immediate response back with texts more than they do with emails. So it can become an invasive burden more than a help. Plus, texts are hard to search back through if you're looking for something you talked about a month or more back. Keep healthy boundaries by requiring clients to submit written changes or requests via email. You don't want texts about work pouring into your after-hours and weekends, or distracting you while working on other projects. As a freelancer, work-life balance can be very hard to compartmentalize. Clients texting you in the middle of the night about a proof is a breach of that. If a client texts you about work, tell them nicely to put it in an email and you'll get back to them soon.

COMMUNICATION BREAKDOWN

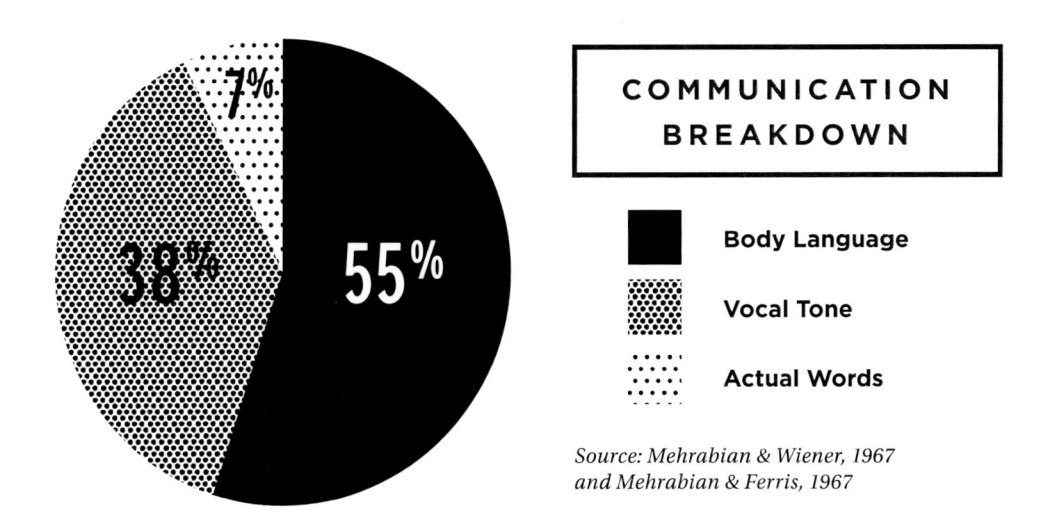

- Body Language: 55%
- Vocal Tone: 38%
- Actual Words: 7%

Source: Mehrabian & Wiener, 1967 and Mehrabian & Ferris, 1967

The Checks and Balances of Verbal and Visual Communication

Over 90% of communication is non-verbal (see the handy graph on this spread for more). It's better to learn early that the soft skills are just as important as the hard skills in business. You might be saying one thing with your words, but your body is giving off a completely different message. Here are some tips for verbal and non-verbal communication.

The Lost Art of Non-Verbal Communication

1. **Look engaged and interested!** This might seem like a duh, but we can't tell you how many interviews we've held over the years at Hoodzpah with candidates who look bored to death. Ways to show you're engaged: Smile. Nod when a good point is made. Laugh when a joke is made (even if it's a lame one). Don't tap your fingers or bounce your feet. When someone else is talking, think about your face. You don't have to hold a perma-grin, but you definitely don't want to have a "WTF are you talking about" face on. Only Abercrombie & Fitch models from the 2000s can win sales from "Resting Fitch Face".

2. **Make eye contact.** You don't have to stare the other person down, but if you don't make eye contact you'll come off as shifty, insincere, or uninterested.

3. **Sit up straight:** Lean in. Don't lean back in your chair or slouch. When you're Tina Fey and you run the show, *then* you can lean back.

4. **Walk tall and with purpose.** Don't scoot, scurry, or shlump. When a client is paying you the big bucks they want a confident and capable employee. Sure, the main way you prove this is in your work, but being confident and assured in how you carry yourself helps put your clients at ease too.

5. **Smile.** It's good for you, and good for your clients and peers. British researchers found that one smile can stimulate the brain as much as up to 2,000 chocolate bars; and can be as stimulating as receiving up to 16,000 Pounds Sterling in cash (around $22,000). Smiles are linked to reward centers in our brains, which release "happy hormones". And smiles are contagious. So when you smile, it triggers your client to smile, and soon you're both on your way down a happy hormone spiral that's good for everyone. Don't get us wrong, a winning smile doesn't compensate for poor work ethic or skill. But it can enhance your skills by tying your brand to a positive human experience.

6. **For heaven's sake, give a firm hand shake.**

Verbal Communcation

1. **Speak with passion.** Show excitement through voice modulation. You are not a robot. Let your enthusiasm out of the cage. You don't have to fake it. But don't hide that light under a basket.

2. **Speak clearly.** Ar-tic-u-late. No mumblers allowed. If you're prone to talking fast, try to slow yourself down. It's not only helpful for your listener, it also allows you time to navigate your thoughts as you respond.

3. **Avoid these words:** Um; Like (if not in a simile); Kind of; Sort of; Stuff; I guess; Curse words (read your audience on this one).

4. **Don't try to use big words to sound smart.** Big words don't make you smart—Clear, well thought out ideas do. Speak in a way that is natural to you, and that the client can understand. Talking over your client's head might make you seem pompous.

5. **Don't interrupt.**

6. **Don't pretend to understand if you don't.** Ask questions to clarify if you need to.

7. **Don't get defensive.** Take ideas and constructive criticism graciously. You are not an island, and most of your career will be spent working in conjunction with others. You're likely to have differing opinions. Make time for critique with your clients and collaborators. If you know when it is happening, and what goal you are working toward, you can mentally prepare yourself and make a case for your decisions. Listen before responding, and try to base your responses on facts rather than emotions.

8. **Most importantly: Listen first.** Shut up and listen. Gather as many facts and context clues from your audience before you open your mouth. Then, when you talk, you can tie your conclusions or thoughts to what has already been said to include your listener and build common ground.

Visually Defining Your Terms with Mood Boards

When dealing with clients, words are some of our main means of communication, but words can unintentionally deceive. Inadvertently, one word can mean many different things depending on who is saying it. Personal preference and experience fill that word with a unique definition for each person. Generally, we all know what "modern" means, but what does it mean specifically when your client says they want a modern website or a modern logo? Listening is the first step. Let the client explain to you what they mean by further describing and giving examples. Then interpret. A picture is worth a thousand words. Create a mood board with your client with visual examples of "modern." Now you are visually and verbally on the same page. You and your client are building a shared and mutually-understood terminology. Plus, a client-approved mood board helps get your client back on track when they start to get distracted throughout the process. It's easy to forget original goals.

Presenting a Proof

When presenting proofs to clients, show that your solution meets your mutual goals for the project. Use the client's own words in your presentation.

"You explained to me that X was a goal for this logo. This logo meets that goal because of Y and Z."

Also, go the extra mile to contextualize your work when possible. Your creative process can be thwarted by subjective opinions from clients. We've all heard these infuriating words from a client before, "I just don't like it, I don't know why." Your best shot for avoiding subjective and emotional client feedback like this is to make the research and project proofs analytical and specific. Always show how the work you did directly relates back to your approved mood boards and core project goal. If you can prove your work aligns with these things, then a client's subjective feedback becomes irrelevant in the face of facts. If your client is smart, they won't let their personal biases detract from a proof that meets the project goals and best serves their target demographic.

Treat your proof presentation analytically. Know what you're willing to compromise on in the proofs. What are non-crucial elements of the work that are open to change or could be removed? Be flexible with the client on those things. Doctors don't let patients choose how they set a broken bone, but they do let them choose the color of the cast. What are project-crucial features that you're willing to fight for? Be ready to make a case for those.

---

*

HOODZPAH HOT-TAKE

RE: CLIENT REVISIONS

Know what you're willing to compromise on and what you're ready to fight for... Doctors don't let patients choose how they set a broken bone, but they do let them choose the color of the cast.

For the sake of the client, for the sake of the project, and for the sake of your portfolio. You're a professional, and clients are hiring you to help steer them in these decisions. Remember that. And then remember that your client is also a professional. If they can make a better case for why the creative work should be changed, they deserve an equally analytical response from you.

Our friend Bayan Joonam (formerly of SoulPancake) once shared a helpful exercise with us: Before each client proposal or proof review, he personally anticipates any questions or reasons the client might say "no" to his idea/proof. Then he writes down his best answers to those sticking points. Poking holes in your own plan may seem strange; but by considering all the possible problems, you can shore up your argument. You'll be able to answer their questions before they even have a chance to ask them. This extra prep will also help you avoid defensive or emotional responses to a client's feedback. Consider their "ifs", "ands" and "buts" (not butts) from every angle, and know how to address them.

We Just Disagree

Sometimes, despite best efforts, you cannot get on the same page as a client. You and your client might seem to agree on overall project goals and aesthetic direction, but when you show them progress proofs they are unhappy or unsure about the results. You show how your work aligns with original mood boards and goals, but they still are unhappy or unconvinced.

"I just don't like it" is not a valid response to a proof that meets the requirement you and your client have agreed on for success. At that point you have to be honest with them. Some helpful things to tell a wishy-washy client:

- "The work I have done meets the project goals that we outlined and approved together at the very beginning. We did that to have a means to measure success. Based on our original criteria, this is successful. See how my proof is in line with our mood board…"

- "It might not be your personal preference, but you can be happy to know that this will work for the target demographic and project for these reasons which we outlined in our research phase. Trust the data. We know your audience wants X, Y and Z. This proof delivers on those needs in the following ways…"

- "If you have unlimited time and money, then we can continue down this road and try to make exactly what you 'envision'. But neither of us have that luxury, so let's finalize what we've come up with, which we know meets our goals, even if it's not your 'perfect' ideal. Perfect is the enemy of good. This is a good solution because…"

- "You can pay for more rounds of revisions, but if you can't articulate to me what you want or don't like about this latest proof, then I doubt we'll make much more progress."

- "Let's take our personal opinions out of it and launch this iteration to a test group of your users/audience. If the proof does well with the test group, then we'll have our answer from the voices that matter most: our end user."

- "Based on your feedback, it sounds like our original project goal has changed. Our scope of work was based on a specific goal and style that you signed off on in the research/discovery phase. If you want to change the direction, that's OK, but I'll need to requote you, since the project will be significantly shifting."

If this kind of sound reasoning doesn't work, you might have to cut ties with the client. You cannot help someone who cannot articulate helpful feedback, changes their mind on a whim, or ignores tried and proven solutions. Try and end the relationship as positively as possible, and according to your contract terms. Get paid for what is owed you, and then give the client any work owed them.

Saying No is Okay

As a professional, it's your right and your duty to say "no" when you think it's in the best interest of your client and project. Save your objections for project-crucial decisions, like we mentioned before. Don't let your personal bias turn you into a grumpy collaborator. The client has rights to decision making. But if you fear a decision could derail the project success, be vocal about it calmly and analytically. If the client ignores your protests, you have to make a choice: follow the client's instructions despite your qualms, or terminate the project early.

Breaking Up with Clients is Allowed

There are times when the only move you have is to end a project early. This is where a clear and flexible termination clause in your contract comes in handy. If you want to end a client relationship, don't just go radio silent without any notice. Contracts need to be formally terminated in writing, usually. You need confirmation that the client has received your notice. No matter what reason your client relationship ends, remember that you are still owed for work completed. Invoice for any outstanding work, and send any partially completed work, if that is something you have agreed to do in your contract (we don't agree to this if someone cancels a branding or logo project early, but for most other projects we're fine sending working files). Consult with your business lawyer on how best to handle the project breakup. You don't want to give the client any grounds to sue you (for breach of duty or otherwise).

Client indecision could be one reason to end things. Here are some other valid reasons for calling it quits:

- **Harassment:** When there is a breakdown of mutual respect. Drama is great on TV, but not in your work relationships. If clients are verbally or physically abusive, or cannot respect professional boundaries, you need to end the relationship.

- **Time Issues:** When a client is stalling a project so much that it is cutting into your schedule for other clients. We've had people fail to respond to us for months. After 30 days of non-response, it's more than fair to ask a client to settle up what is owed. Give them a heads up that if they continue to delay, you'll have to terminate the project, because you have other clients you've scheduled. This term should be mentioned in your contracts if you want to have this move available to you.

- **Money Issues:** When clients have failed to pay you. It's nice to give someone a heads up if a payment is late, and give them a chance to make it right. But if they are chronically avoiding your requests for settlement, then stop all work. If they refuse to pay what is owed for the work you've done, then do not give them any project files until they do. If they already have possession of your work, consider a cease and desist letter. Likely, your copyright or licensing terms only stipulate that the client is allowed to use your work if they have paid for the services. This means the client is infringing on your copyright if they have not paid for the work which they are using.

- **Butting Heads:** When you and the client just cannot get along. Your personalities clash and neither of you is enjoying the process.

- **Tragedy:** When something unexpected comes up in you or your client's life, and you/they are physically or emotionally no longer able to fulfil responsibilities. Be sure your contract allows for this kind of termination, in case you need it. Tragedy can strike without warning, and you don't want a lawsuit looming over your head just because you need to take a step back from your business. Be very careful on how you bow out. Try and replace your position if you can. Refer them to a trusted colleague who can continue the work. At the very least, alert your client to your situation as soon as possible, so they have enough time to find someone to pick up the work.

MAY YOU BE Healthy

Wealthy & Wise

12

Taxes, Accounting, and Measuring Financial Health

Keeping your green in the green.

———

We've talked about managing individual projects, but in this chapter we're going to zoom out and take a macro look at managing your overall business finances and health. In short, keeping the taxes paid, the invoices sent, the accounts in the green, and the business growing. Some of these things will be more unique to those of you living in the United States (the tax bits), but there's also some good across-the-board advice for measuring and analyzing your business's success. So run all these things by your own accountant and financial advisor to work out a plan suited for you.

Tackle Bookkeeping and Accounting

What's the Difference Between Accounting and Bookkeeping?

Bookkeeping: Recording financial transactions. Examples: creating invoices, making a record of money coming into your account from projects, and of money going out of your account for expenses and payroll.

Accounting: Analyzing your financial transactions, reporting the summary to the government when needed, and drawing conclusions on your overall financial health. Examples: completing your business taxes, creating reports and statements that reveal insights about your business and finances, using bookkeeping data to advise you about financial decisions.

In many situations, a business owner can handle their own bookkeeping with the help of great software. But they're less likely to be able to fulfill the role of an accountant. You'll definitely want to hire a CPA (Certified Public Accountant) at least once a year to help you file your taxes from the previous year, analyze the health of your business, and help you plan for the next year of business (including estimated taxes). You might need their assistance here and there in between, as well. Once you find a great CPA, hold on for dear life, showering them with gifts and praise. Great CPAs get busy fast. Having one who is with you for the long haul, and understands your financial history, is valuable.

Get Started with Accounting and Bookkeeping Software

With accounting software, you can create customized and branded invoices, receive payments online, track profit and loss with the click of a button, record expenses and income, and more. Most accounting software is cloud-based, meaning you can do it on your laptop or even from your phone, so long as you have internet. Most are subscription priced. The cost is usually very reasonable considering the incredible value. Some are even completely free!

If you are diligent and willing to apply yourself to learning an accounting software, like so many small business owners do every year, you can save some money on a bookkeeper. There are so many software options out there that make the task fairly intuitive. Ask your CPA which accounting software they recommend. Then ask if you can pay them to setup the basics of your books in the software. If they don't have time, you can also hire a bookkeeper to get you started. They might even give you a run through of how to use the platform before you take over. All software has a Support or FAQ page with easy tutorials, too. If all else fails, head to YouTube (AKA ye fount of eternal wisdom).

Below are some accounting software options popular now. Research them to see which, if any, of these options is best for you:

a. **Wave (freemium):** www.WaveApps.com

b. **Freshbooks:** www.Freshbooks.com

c. **Xero:** www.Xero.com

d. **Quickbooks Online:** www.Quickbooks.intuit.com

e. **And Co (freemium):** www.And.co. This is an interesting option helping freelancers do more than just basic invoicing and reports. The platform also helps you create contracts and time track.

Once you have chosen your software method, record and update your expenses and income regularly. With most online software subscriptions you can connect to your business bank accounts (through a secure internet-based bank feed) and import expenses and income automatically. Then you reconcile the imported bank statements with the income and expenses you have recorded in your accounting software, to make sure everything is matching up and itemized. Schedule regular time slots weekly or monthly to reconcile your books so you can easily remember what the automatically synced bank transactions are for. If you wait too long, an unfamiliar expense is hard to reconcile.

Being intimately aware of your business finances will help you track the health and growth of your business in between meetings with your accountant. Without a healthy cash flow and a good financial standing, your small business can fast become one of the biggest regrets of your life. Stay on top of it. If you see your expenses start to get too high, you can quickly alter your spending habits before you get in the hole.

If, after trying to do your own bookkeeping, you find that you are making costly errors or don't have the time to spend on it, then consider paying someone to do it for you. Saving money by doing it yourself only saves you money if you do it properly. There's no shame in delegating.

---

*

HOODZPAH
HOT-TAKE

Saving money by doing it yourself only saves you money if you do it properly. There's no shame in delegating.

Keep Records

Record keeping is part of running a smooth business. It's crucial come tax time. Realistically speaking, what records should you keep and for how long? "Record retention" is a term for how long you keep official information on hand according to the SBA, FDIC and U.S. Financial Literacy and Education Commission. In their *Money Smart for a Small Business Curriculum: Record Keeping for a Small Business* they say, "The Internal Revenue Service (IRS) determines some record retention guidelines. Other retention requirements are legal in nature, such as what may be required by contract with those you do business with. Expert recommendations vary. Also, retention schedules vary by region. For example, a state may have a different statute of limitation for legal liability (law suits). Check with your attorney for legal requirements. Check with your accountant for financial-related requirements."

When we say "records," we mean keeping proof that something happened. Keeping a copy of a form you file, or a scan of a check you send, or a paid receipt of an online order. Here's a general guide of what records to keep and for how long. As noted, the requirements can vary by region or industry, so check with your accountant and attorney (especially if you're outside of the United States).

Record to keep	For how long
Invoices and receivables	5 years
Checks and payables	5 years
Auditors reports	Always
Annual statements	Always
Payroll	6 years
Personnel contracts	4-5 years
Personnel files	3 years
Insurance records	5 years
Client contracts and copyright information	Always
Licenses and permits	As required
Tax returns	Always
Employee withholding	7 years
Tax bills and statements	Always
1099s	Always

Anticipate Taxes

Pay Estimated Taxes

Please. Don't. Overlook. This. This will save you a lot of shock and horror at the end of the year (providing you make a net gain). As a freelancing creative who is contracted out by other businesses, your state and federal taxes are up to you to make good on. What many freelancers realize too late, is that they are required to pay estimated taxes each quarter, not just at the end of the year. Talk to your accountant to get the vouchers you'll need to make the payments, or to setup automatic e-payments. Otherwise, you'll end up with a penalty fee and a huge lump sum of owed taxes when you file your annual return. The SBA explains, "Calculating what you owe each quarter requires figuring out your expected adjusted gross income, taxable income, taxes, deductions, and credits for the year. Each business situation is different, especially if you are a new business owner, so it's worth spending some time with a tax advisor to understand the best calculation method for your situation."

Plan for Annual Taxes

Every time you work with a new client, you should have a current W-9 filled out and ready to send them. We've discussed it before, but it can't hurt to repeat. The W-9 form provides your client with your official business name, tax ID and some other information that they will need for annual tax purposes. If you've made more than $600 from a client in a year, then they will have to report this to the IRS through a Form 1099-Misc. A 1099 is like a freelancer's version of an employee's W-2. You should receive a copy of these forms from clients by the end of January. If you yourself have contracted a freelancer for over $600 of work, you'll also have to prepare a 1099 with your accountant to send to the contractor by the end of January.

When you receive 1099s for the work you have done with clients, double check that the tally of what the client has paid you is accurate. You should have a record of the work you did with them in your own bookkeeping. Keep the form in a safe place and bring it with you when you meet with your accountant to prepare your year-end taxes.

Analyze the Success of Your Business

How's your business doing? Don't leave your business baby to be raised by wolves. Like any new child, it deserves regular check-ups and parental supervision. Here are some ways to measure your success:

Check your profit / loss statement and compare it to previous periods. This shows how much money you're bringing in versus spending within a specific period of time. Run this report every month, and compare it to your previous months. Your goal is to always make a profit by the end of the month. If you have two consecutive months in the red, it's time to re-examine and make some changes. Trim your expenses in any way possible, and analyze why you aren't getting enough income. Are you not getting enough leads? Are you not converting enough quotes? You could also consider adding new services or products to diversify your income. Or is it just a slow month that you need to weather?

Look at a more detailed expense and income statement to see what you are spending the most money on and making the most money on.

1. Are there areas of expenses that are cutting into your profits too much? See if you can cancel any subscriptions or cut back on anything next month to make sure those expenses don't get out of hand.

2. Which of your services are the most popular? Consider raising prices on that service or going after more clients who need that service, since the demand is high.

3. Which services are the least popular? Why is this?

Compare your flat-rate projects to the actual hours spent on them. A $15,000 project sounds great on the surface, but if you're spending too much time on the project, the profit gets lower and lower. When you flat rate projects, time track regardless. Why? So you can do the math at the end and make sure you made a good rate at the end of the day.

Calculate how many of your quotes have been accepted and rejected. Is the acceptance number really high? Consider raising your rates. Are your rejection rates really high? Consider lowering your rates. Or, perhaps you need to invest more time in proving the value of your services when you present your pricing to potential clients. Create presentations that show your successful work for clients in the past. Create educational materials for your potential clients that explain your process so they understand the time and effort involved.

Review the returns you're getting on your advertising and marketing efforts. Make sure that you are getting a good ROI (return on investment) out of your ad buys and marketing work. Give the campaign a fair amount of time to get a read on the results. You can judge ROI quantitatively and qualitatively. Quantitative measures your success off of the quantity of return you get. Qualitative measures by the quality of the return you get. Let's say you spend only $5 on Ad #1. The ad results in 5,000 referrals to your site, but you don't land any jobs from the traffic. It seems like a good deal since you're only spending a low sum to get such high traffic. But if the quality of the viewer isn't interested in your product or able to pay for your level of service, is it really worth it? The SEO boost from the traffic is worth something, but you aren't seeing work from it in the end. You then spend $100 on Ad #2 which results in 200 visits to your site and three new clients who book you for $5,000 projects. Although the initial expense is higher, it's justified because it delivers better quality results. Another example: you hire a social media consultant to help manage your accounts. While she only increases your following slightly, she succeeds in changing the audience perception of your brand. Her posts are engaging your audience better and creating more positive buzz about your business. This is a qualitative result that might not be reflected in the hard stats. So consider all the angles before you cancel a campaign or double down on a marketing effort.

Analyze your web traffic. Install Google Analytics (it's free as of the publication of this book) on your website to gather data about your audience. Is traffic to your site steadily growing? What content is most popular on your site? Consider posting more of that kind of content. What sites are referring the most traffic to you? Those are good places to invest more time and effort. Also look at the analytics on your social media profiles.

Review your personal goals for your company. What are you happy with? What do you feel you need to get better at? Did you meet the goals you set as far as new clients or increased income? If not, why? Are you steadily growing your skills and experience so you can justify higher rates?

Consider alternative revenue streams (services and products). Is there a new type of service that has high demand with little competition in your industry? You can get training in that type of service, or bring someone on to your company (full-time, part-time, or freelance) who can help you in that area. Dare to think outside of services. Services like logo design and photo shoots require your unique time and effort. However, if you can turn your talents into products, there's potential to make money with hundreds and thousands of clients from one investment of time and effort. It's the difference between doing a custom lettering for one client as a service that only they can use, versus creating a font that you can sell as a product to unlimited clients for the same amount of time and effort. You limit your income potential when you limit your earnings to hours worked for services rendered. Don't get us wrong, both services and products have their place and unique advantages, though. With a font you'd have to sell many more licenses to make the same amount of profit you would on one custom lettering project. Diversify your company offering and you can reap the benefits of both. Be smart about how you productize your talents. Your products should never undercut the value of your services. For example, if you sell a licensable logo pack on a site like Creative Market for $20, will it make your clients hesitant to pay you thousands of dollars for a custom logo? Optimally, your product will enhance your services and build your brand equity.

Check in with a business mentor. Getting an outside perspective is a healthy exercise. Whether the person knows you, or knows your industry, they can offer fresh advice. You know some things, but you don't know everything. Surround yourself with people smarter than you.

Write down your biggest stresses and ideate ways to alleviate or avoid them. Usually a reoccurring annoyance can be righted with a change in your procedure or structure. Taking a few minutes to weigh the pros and cons can give you the clarity to make changes that ease your burden. We often turn auto-pilot on and forget that there is room for optimization in how we do business.

Chapter Checklist: To Do

- [ ] Pick your accounting software and connect your business bank account feed. Learn to reconcile the synced income and expenses. (Ask your CPA for help or Google it.)

- [ ] Make a "Records" folder on your computer. This is where you'll store important records.

- [ ] Talk with your CPA about quarterly estimated tax payments and annual tax planning.

- [ ] Once you've got your bookkeeping up to date in your accounting software, run a Profit & Loss Statement. Get familiar with other reports offered within the software.

- [ ] Write down your business goals for the year.

- [ ] Ideate on alternative revenue streams.

- [ ] Write down the names of business-savvy friends (in or out of your industry). Ask them to lunch or coffee. Reach out to just say "hi" via email or text. Take care of those relationships. One might evolve into a mentorship for you.

- [ ] Write down pain points in your business right now. Ideate on people or processes that could help alleviate the stress.

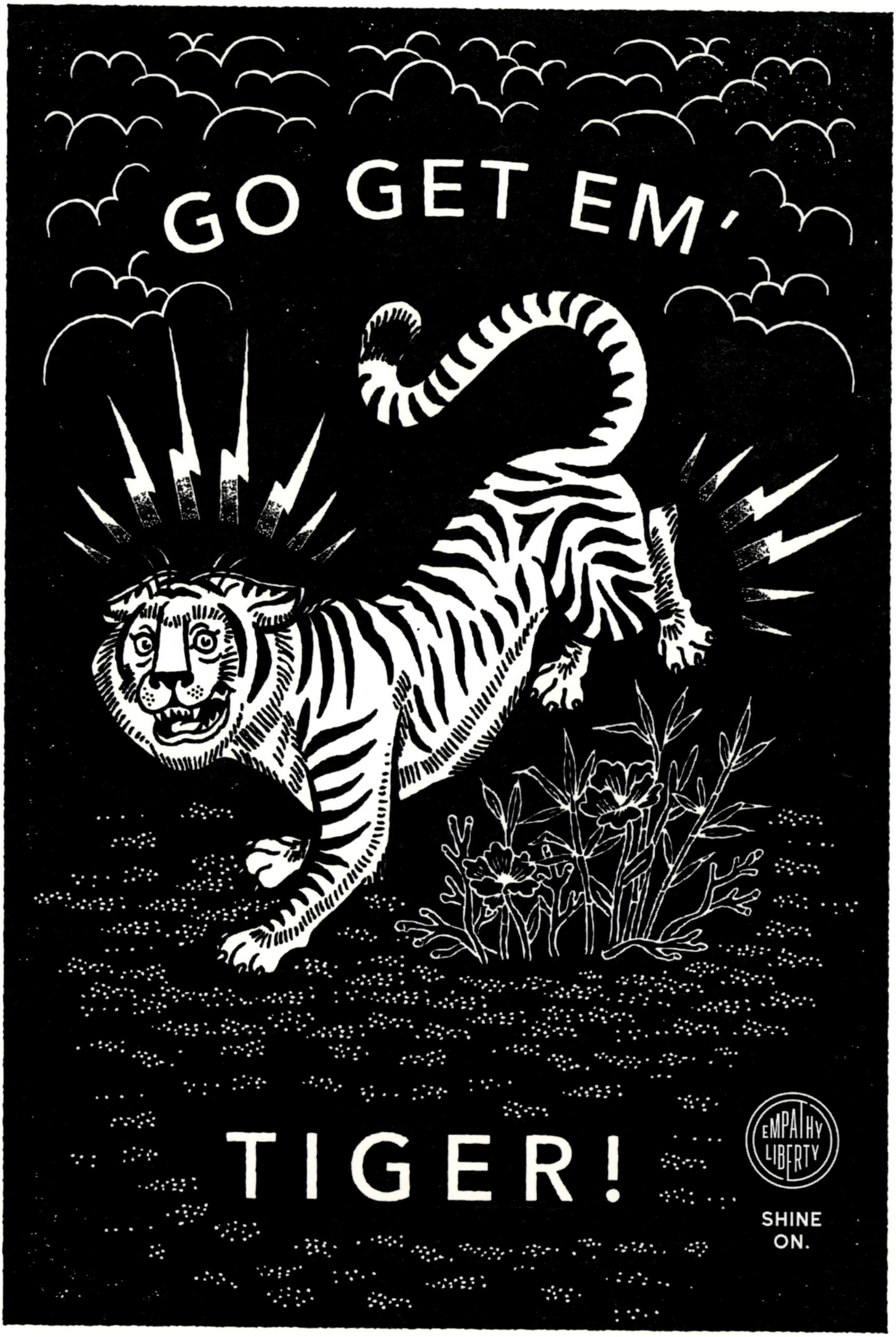
GO GET EM'
TIGER!
EMPATHY LIBERTY
SHINE ON.

13

Staying Competitive and Adaptive

Keep on keeping on.

———

Whatever you do, don't lose touch with your industry or the world at large. You're going to go through phases in your career where you feel like you've lost your edge, or lost interest; like you're washed up, like the industry and trends have changed and left you behind. When that day comes, give yourself a hug and then snap out of it. Get out there and dig into new methods, movements, and technologies. Attend a conference to broaden your sphere of peers and influences. Do something completely outside of your profession to give you a new creative outlet. Just don't blame it on the era or the industry.

The creative world has always been a competitive and demanding one, even before Twitter trolls and the scathing Medium think-piece became a thing. Surviving as a creative is the same as surviving in life: gather data, iterate, adapt, repeat. They're the lessons we've been learning in design school classrooms and conference halls for years. Losing touch with your creative community, the mentality of your consumer, the sentiments of the world, or the methods of your industry is death to your business.

Staying Adaptive

Challenge your ideas and test your assumptions on the regular. We all have inherent bias. Welcome feedback that doesn't align with your ideology or background. To think you have figured everything out is to miss out. The more you learn, the more reference you have for balanced conclusions, and the more you have to bring to the table, no matter who your client is, or what their business is. You're never too old, experienced, or awesome to learn something new.

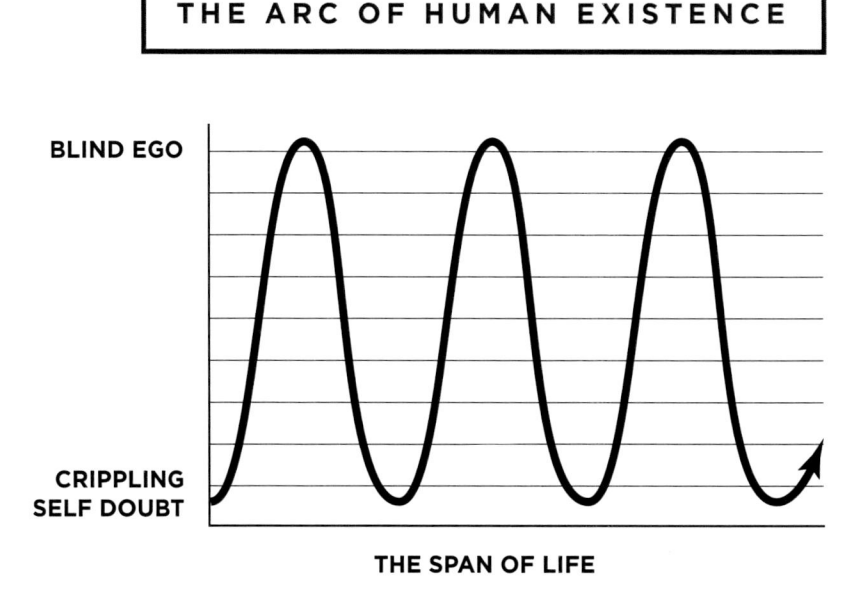

THE ARC OF HUMAN EXISTENCE

BLIND EGO

CRIPPLING SELF DOUBT

THE SPAN OF LIFE

If you'll look at the graph on the previous page you'll see the natural arc of human existence. A roller-coaster of ups and downs between blind ego and crippling self-doubt. We're the worst judge when it comes to ourselves because of our manic perceptions, biases, insecurities, and ideals. Rarely do we sit comfortably in a balanced state of confidence and adaptability. We barely passed high school Biology, but let's review a few truths about how our brains are wired.

Science Says You're Addicted to Being Right

According to research studies, when you are found to be right in a situation, or are given validation in your opinion, the reward center of your brain lights up, similar to the way it would if you were getting high off drugs. Like any drug, confirmation bias impairs judgement, and it can be an addicting high. We seek that feeling again and again.

As we continue to hone our craft and elevate our skill, we are confirmed and rewarded for a job well-done more and more. This confirmation triggers those addictive reward responses in our brain. We continue to chase that high of being right. No one wants to be wrong or to be embarrassed by a mistake. It's a natural desire to win rather than lose. As we get further into our professional careers, especially as self-employed creatives, we encounter less and less healthy ego checks and critique. As children and teens we were regularly corrected and critiqued by teachers and parents as we learned and grew. Once we graduate from schools and move away from family, that accountability dwindles as we start embracing our independence. This can be an exciting time of discovery. But if we're not still looking for feedback and critique from people in our evolving lives, it's easy to start thinking that we're above it all. That we're untouchable. We know more than our peers. Our clients are dumb. Our boss doesn't understand our art. The world is stupid. Therefore, they don't deserve our respect or our ear. We can be addicted to the idea that we're always right, and anything wrong that happens is always someone else's fault. Left unchecked, this addiction to confirming one's own opinions can lead seemingly capable people to eventually say or do contextually or socially unaware things. You can fall from public grace real fast when you're so high on your own bias that you act insensitively or rashly.

Naturally, we don't like to be in these situations. This fear of being wrong (and its cousin, fear of being found out to be lacking, a.k.a. Imposter Syndrome) can lead us to surround ourselves with people who are just like us. Then we really make misinformed decisions based on fear and isolationism. This is how dictators rule. They cut their country off from the free flow of information, avoiding any contradiction to their own way of life. What results is a suffocating bubble. Instead of forward progress because of an influx of fresh, new ideas and innovation, they end up getting left behind, a society stuck in time. In instances like that it's just a matter of time before the revolution. Why impose this same kind of mentality on your own life and creative work? We think it goes without saying, but heck, we'll say it: don't be a creative Stalin.

You Might Be a Creative Dictator if...

1. **You Create a Cave of Isolation:** It's how every *Forensic Files* episode plays out: new lovers meet, a fiery romance ensues, and soon infatuation leads to isolationism. They only have eyes for each other, alienating family and friends. They spend every waking hour together, becoming jealous and possessive, not wanting to share their person with anyone else. Soon the things they love about each other become the things they loathe about each other. And then *murder*. It's the same in creativity! Holding an idea too tight, and not sharing it to sharpen it, leads to a dead idea, or at the very least, a stale one. **Anti-Tyrant Solution:** Seek community, online and offline. Seek new relationships with people of different backgrounds and ways of thinking. Enlist some friends, kin, and/or colleagues to be the accountability partners that call you on your bullshit when you're drinking a 64 ounce Big Gulp of your own Kool-Aid. Share your work regularly online. When strangers give negative feedback in a less than delicate way, remember that divine messages sometimes come from the mouths of asses. Just because it's abrasive doesn't mean it's without any shred of insight.

2. **You Fear Transparency:** You're afraid to disclose your process, techniques, and knowledge. **Anti-Tyrant Solution:** To start, find a group of peers you can spit ball with openly and without fear. Maybe even invoke a cone of silence clause (all information shared is not to leave the circle) to promote honesty and openness. You don't have to tell the whole world every detail of your business, but you should be looking to get regular feedback, as well as find ways to share your own wisdom with others. Besides seeking feedback from people you admire and trust, make yourself available to broader critique by sharing your thoughts publicly. The Renaissance that occurred between the 14th and 17th centuries was an explosion of creativity, discovery, and understanding. This boom was spurred in part thanks to the invention of printing, which allowed people to share their studies and works on a broad scale; along with an intellectual movement called Humanism that encouraged shared wisdom, free inquiry and criticism. Inspire a revival of creativity by promoting shared knowledge.

3. **You use Emotional or Subjective Reasoning to Justify Choices.** As twins, we have to be really careful of this one. Working with family can be tough. Critique sessions can quickly descend into emotionally charged fights stemming from unresolved issues that are unrelated (like how Amy always got the top bunk). The same can happen in any working relationship. Nancy's opinion isn't valid because she listens to pop country and she beat you out for captain of the company softball team. Joe doesn't know anything because he microwaves leftover fish at lunch and roots for the Patriots. Just because y'all aren't best friends, doesn't mean their opinions are any less valid. **Anti-Tyrant Solution:** When it comes to making work related decisions, weigh all choices against whether they support or detract from the one clear goal of your project at hand. This is where the research phase becomes very important. Knowing the main goal of the project, who it needs to serve, and what the terms are for success will help you

make clear cut decisions based on those facts rather than on your personal preference. Consider that maybe there isn't only one right solution to your problem. Right can be relative depending on your upbringing, personal history, and world view. Leave room for different perspectives.

4. **You Banish Rivals:** If someone disagrees with you, is your first inclination to retreat or ice them out? Do you purposefully avoid working with collaborators or clients whom you think might challenge you? Just because someone doesn't 100% agree with you doesn't mean you can't have a respectful and professional work experience (or friendship).
Anti-Tyrant Solution: Try to find understanding in why someone feels the way they do. Reserve judgement until you've really heard them. Of course, there's a difference between healthy dialogue and straight harassment. You don't have to endure foolish people who just like to spew negativity for the sake of havoc, just don't silence every voice that doesn't harmonize with yours. Opposing questions will either poke holes in an undercooked idea, or strengthen the resolve of a great solution.

Hey You, You Can't Control Everything

It can be really hard to cope when change happens that's outside our control. But change is inevitable. A career ending, a project failing, a new technology replacing our skill set, and so on. If you were a marketing creative pre-internet, much of your life's knowledge and gut instinct became irrelevant when the internet hit. What's right today could be wrong tomorrow. Keep your eyes open and never assume that life as we know it now is the way it will continue to be. Try to find anchors in your life that provide value and meaning outside of your work. You are more than your work. You need purpose beyond your work to have the strength to adapt. Seek sources of joy and contentment outside of your work.

Staying Competitive

Stay up to Date

Keep up to date on evolving technology and new programs in your area of expertise. Don't be afraid of new programs and software. Advancements in technology will likely make the tedious parts of your job easier! Or at the very least, technology's remaining limitations will remind people why we still need real people like you at the helm.

Be aware of creative trends and aesthetic evolutions, trying to decipher what's passing and what's lasting. If you want to master a new style, give yourself an assignment. Participate in a 30-day creative challenge, or create a poster for your Uncle Bill's cover band. Just make time to play and try new things. Keep advancing your skills by investing in ongoing education, whether that's through online courses, mentorship, or otherwise. Continue to adapt your methods based on your ever-increasing experience. In short, never stop learning and growing.

Invest in Community

Get hooked in to your local creative scene. Contributing to your local community (i.e. meet-ups, industry associations, lectures, etc.) will promote alliances with peers who understand your struggle and can offer mentorship or advice. If you're in a small or remote area with no creative hub, look online for a community. Dribbble, Twitter, Twitch...there are so many ways to meet people. The hard part is playing an active role. Wherever you go, commit to engage.

Look for ways to lend your talent and time to making your non-creative community better, too, whether locally or globally. This will lead to positive ties between your business and the community. Whatever you do, don't fall into the habit of hermiting away in your home or office with only your backlog of podcasts and your cases of LaCroix to keep you warm. Get out in the world. Go out and have fun for the hell of it. Invest in relationships. It will generally make for a more enriched existence, and that will translate to a more productive and gratifying work life in turn. Make a conscious effort to pursue new relationships with people from different industries, life stages, and neighborhoods. Faceted life experiences lend to a more well-rounded and powerful perspective for your creative work and business.

Seek Inspiration in the Unfamiliar

This sounds easy, but it's not. We're not talking about scrolling through Pinterest for an hour a day. We're talking about eyes-on, hands-on, out-of-the-box, creative challenges. Get a hobby outside of what you do every day for a living. Something where you can unwind from pointing and clicking. Something new that challenges you to grow your creativity in unchartered ways. Take breaks. Take vacations. Go on adventures. This doesn't mean you have to hop on a plane to Stockholm (although that's cool!). There's adventure all around us. Instead of going to the same coffee shop you always go to, try a new one in a different part of town. Take a new detour home. You'll be amazed at all the things you didn't even know existed. Look up hikes and trails in your area.

Beauty and inspiration are all around you. Sometimes the simplest deviations from your routine can expose you to something magical and new, leading to a new way of thinking, possibly resulting in a revelation about how to solve a problem. You don't want to spend so much time working that you have no time for absorbing the new and unexpected (they said into the mirror to themselves). Without this inlet of fresh water, you'll get stagnant. Stagnation breeds frustration and frustration breeds resentment. Resentful people see the world as the enemy instead of the proverbial oyster.

Farewell for now....

You did it! You finished this book! It was a lot of work, and you've hopefully come away with a lot of applicable knowledge and actionable next steps. But remember this one last thing: none of that knowledge counts for anything if you're not applying it. Just start. Today. You're probably thinking of a million reasons why you're not ready, why now isn't a good time for you, why you can't. But let's be clear, you can. And since there's never the "right time", there's no better time than right now.

Go get 'em tiger!

Amy Hood and Jen Hood

Do you have more questions? Want to tell us what you loved / hated / LOL-ed over in this book? Tweet at us using the hashtag #FABAS and tag @HoodzpahDesign. We're also on Instagram! Tag ya girls.